Curandero Therapy

A Holistic Approach to Healing

ROSA M LUNA

DEDICATION

I would like to dedicate this book to all those who are willing and able to broaden their horizons in an effort to help others, and to the Latinos, Native Americans and others who seek help and healing through alternative healing modalities such as Curanderismo and Reiki methodologies. I believe in the importance of supporting humanity by embracing the various methods by which they can be healed according to their culture. Thank you for keeping an open mind as I share the basis of Curandero Therapy. .

CONTENTS

INTRODUCTION

Greetings, my name is Rosa M. Luna, and I am a practitioner of Curandero Therapy. With a background in folk healing, I hold the designation of Reiki Master and serve as an instructor in Curandero Therapy. Additionally, I am a certified Clinical Hypnosis Therapist, bringing a wealth of experience to my practice spanning three decades, where I have assisted individuals facing a diverse range of challenges.

Curandero Therapy involves the treatment of individuals grappling with fears, curses, obsolete belief systems, and various unresolved emotional issues. I embarked on this journey over 30 years ago, inheriting the healing methods from my mother, who was also a skilled Curandera. Her reputation drew people from considerable distances to seek her guidance, a testament to her effectiveness in the absence of modern advertising methods.

The practice evolved organically, relying on the powerful mechanism of "word of mouth." Despite my transition to a metropolitan area, the demand for my services persisted. Juggling a full-time role as a mental health professional for the State, I found individuals lining up at my residence after work hours, necessitating a streamlined scheduling process.

In managing the increased demand, I facilitated appointments for those who could not be accommodated immediately, ensuring that the treatment process remained efficient. Some clients required urgent medical attention, and I took it upon myself to accompany them to the hospital, providing interpretation services and advocating for their needs.

Recognizing the financial constraints of some individuals, I introduced a unique approach where they could compensate with offerings such as fruits, particularly during the cherry season in Oregon, where I resided. The community's generosity extended to other produce, homemade delicacies, and thoughtful gestures, contributing to a supportive and nurturing atmosphere during consultations.

These moments of shared kindness, whether through flowers, fresh produce, or homemade goods, became integral to the consultation experience. I deeply valued these gestures, acknowledging the thoughtfulness of those who recognized the demands of my dual roles and extended their generosity in various forms.

Luna Institute of Curanderos

Established in 2002, the Luna Institute of Curanderos was founded with the purpose of providing training in the ancient tradition of alternative healing methods. Recognizing the financial constraints faced by many immigrants and those working in agricultural careers, who often turn to herbalists or village doctors for traditional medicine, the institute has aimed to impart healing skills drawn from diverse traditions worldwide.

The overarching goal remains the re-establishment of the Luna Institute of Curanderos, serving as a center for educating individuals on healing practices rooted in the talents of healers across the globe. The vision involves cultivating a community of students who will become healers and educators, preserving and perpetuating traditional healing approaches.

In response to the growing need for culturally sensitive mental health care, the institute endeavors to address the disparities in mental health diagnoses, particularly among the Latino population. Past experiences as an interpreter revealed instances of misdiagnoses and inappropriate medication prescriptions, prompting the realization of the importance of training psychologists in various Latino cultures.

Recent insights from a New York Times editorial underscore the "Hispanic Paradox," drawing attention to the resilience and longevity of Hispanic Americans despite adversity. The Luna Institute of Curanderos intends to harness this strength by incorporating cultural knowledge from diverse healers, offering housing for visiting teachers, and actively supporting the local community.

The institute's mission extends beyond cultural competence in mental health care, encompassing the broader goals of reaching people of all nationalities and contributing to global healing efforts. The convergence of curanderismo and ethno-psychotherapy is recognized, with an emphasis on cultural definitions rather than functional distinctions.

While acknowledging the role of psychiatrists as medical doctors, the institute emphasizes the cultural foundation of curanderos in addressing mental health issues. The intention is to provide personalized, one-on-one sessions with clients, extending support to their families as part of a holistic healing approach.

Amidst the challenges posed by the pandemic, the Luna Institute of Curanderos remains committed to its mission of fostering a better world and contributing to the end of the global health crisis. The institute encourages individuals to seek the guidance of a Curandero Therapist as they work towards collective healing and positive change.

1 CURANDERO THERAPY IS SOMETHING DIFFERENT

Curandero Therapy offers a distinctive and enlightening therapeutic experience, introducing counseling and healing methodologies that diverge from conventional training. Embracing this approach entails broadening one's horizons to enhance the ability to assist others, particularly those from indigenous and diverse cultural backgrounds. These alternative techniques often resonate well with such communities, but it is crucial to acknowledge that adopting this perspective exposes practitioners to a spectrum of unique and potentially unfamiliar situations.

In the pursuit of understanding the unconventional aspects of Curandero Therapy, it is essential to recognize that individuals may share narratives that, at times, seem surreal. Reflecting on personal encounters with unusual phenomena underscores the intricacies of these experiences. To illustrate, during my childhood, a notable event occurred when my dog, Blackie, communicated with me in Spanish, prompting me to adjust my position as I slept. Subsequently, a seemingly magical interaction with moonlit shadows in my backyard evoked both fear and fascination.

Another instance involved a fortuitous incident where a color crayon unexpectedly popped out of its box, coincidentally saving me from a stray bullet. This seemingly trivial occurrence took on significant importance as it averted potential harm. Such anecdotes emphasize the unexpected nature of events that may initially appear insignificant.

Moreover, sharing an encounter from a late night after a Reiki healing weekend adds a dimension of mystique. Witnessing a figure in my living space, seeking assistance, added a layer of complexity to my experiences. The figure, described as a tall, handsome individual in distinctive attire, conveyed a request for help that was unfortunately declined due to exhaustion.

In fostering an open dialogue, I invite others to share their unexplainable or peculiar experiences, as these anecdotes contribute to a richer understanding of the diverse and enigmatic aspects of our existence. Curandero Therapy serves as a conduit for exploring such phenomena and provides a platform for individuals to connect over shared experiences and reflections.

What do you know about intuition?

We all possess an inherent sense of intuition, a capability that some individuals cultivate more consistently than others. Consider instances such as driving down the freeway, where an intuitive feeling prompts a decision to slow down, subsequently avoiding a potential encounter with law enforcement. In reflecting on such moments, one may ponder the source of this intuitive guidance, attributing it to spiritual entities like spirit guides, angels, God, or a broader spiritual source.

An analogous scenario involves the intuitive recognition of a caller before answering a cell phone. This phenomenon, often dismissed as coincidence, underscores the innate potential of intuition. With dedicated practice, individuals can refine and amplify this innate ability. Many people cultivate a strong connection with their spiritual guides, trusting in the accuracy of the guidance they receive.

Intuition manifests in diverse ways, such as accurately guessing outcomes or details seemingly beyond one's immediate knowledge. A notable example involves a friend who demonstrated an exceptional ability to predict individuals' weights on a television show. His precise guesses, attributed to his spiritual companions or spirit guides, showcased the potential depth of intuitive insights.

Exploring this further, the ability to receive specific information through intuition may be heightened in critical or serious matters. As a healer, I have personally experienced the role of intuition in addressing clients' concerns. During healing sessions, I call upon a specific guide dedicated to assisting with intuitive insights.

In one instance, a client shared dreams of wartime experiences, expressing a desire to know about a lost friend's well-being. During the session, I received a vivid vision in my mind's eye—a man dying in the client's arms.

When I relayed this information, the client confirmed that he had indeed lost several friends in the war, with only one having died in his arms. This exchange emphasized the profound and accurate nature of intuitive insights, leaving the client understandably curious about the source of this knowledge.

In essence, the cultivation and utilization of intuition, particularly in healing practices, highlight the potential for meaningful connections with spiritual guides and the valuable insights they can provide.

Preparation for a healing session

As I commence the healing process, I invoke a prayer directed to my spirit guides, angels, and the universal source, encompassing both God and mother God. In this sacred undertaking, I humbly request their presence, seeking to be utilized as a conduit for healing to benefit my fellow individuals. My appeal is for their guidance in facilitating the highest good for those undergoing the healing process, directing their intervention in a manner most conducive to the recipients' well-being. Subsequently, I entreat my guides to establish a connection with the angels and spirit guides of my clients, enabling a collaborative effort between the spiritual entities.

The inherent truthfulness of spirit guides, both yours and mine, stands in contrast to the capacity for falsehood within human interactions. Confronted with instances where clients may provide inaccurate information, I exercise discretion, opting to rephrase questions rather than directly accusing them of dishonesty. I convey that the information received does not align with my spiritual guidance, fostering an atmosphere conducive to openness and truthfulness.

Following these interactions, I purify my healing space through smudging, ensuring a harmonious environment. Subsequently, I offer prayers for the health and healing of my clients, relying on the steadfastness of my intuition. While I may engage in activities such as participating in television games, I find that these external stimuli do not align with my intuitive processes. Instead, my unwavering trust in my guides fosters a growing sense of confidence, with each interaction reinforcing the reliability of their assistance. Recognizing that intuition is a shared human capability, I emphasize the importance of prayer as a means to seek guidance and support from our respective guides and angels.

Root Cause of Illness

The root cause of illness is unresolved emotional issues. Root causes if not taken care of in the mind, body, and heart turn into an illness, and worse if they stay in the body for too long of a time, it could turn into a disease. The root cause is an emotion stuffed into a tissue, muscle, or organ.

What kind of healing you can get is very essential? Going to a shaman or Curandera/o can help assist with getting to the root cause of what is ailing you If the healer has experience in many of these things, she would find it out easily.

Among other information I can obtain from the patient/client's subconscious mind is the goal of the percentage of the healing outcome. While obtaining this information ask your spirit guides to connect to the clients/patients spirits guide or angels. Ask how many sessions will it take to heal? Does the disease benefit the person? Wisdom and answers are always in your questions.

Ask if they really want to heal and do they want to make a change in their lives. In my experience, some of my clients would like to heal and make changes in their lives but there is a secondary gain to their intention. That is one of the reasons to stay ill, could it be that it's because they are applying for Social Security and need to feel ill until they qualify for S.S. Insurance. Wisdom is always in your questions.

At this discovery, I tell them to come back after they qualified for Social Security benefits. There is always a message you are to learn during these times of an illness and the faster you learn this lesson the faster you will heal.

I had a client who had bad knees, while in my treatment with hypnosis, we found out she was a warrior in some of her past lives, and she would always aim at the enemies' knees to stop them or slow them down.

After bringing this knowledge up the pain in her knee cease the hurt, within two weeks she was better and the pain was gone. It took 2 more sessions for another emotional attack. I met with the client about that painful issue. It had come along piggyback on the last healing.

Other questions you could ask is "if the illness is been used as an excuse not to: for example, find a job, get into a relationship, or any other reason not to comply with something that scares them or makes it difficult for themselves to go on, move on with life.

Also judging experiences, good or bad experiences create blockages, as well. Some experiences we judge as a bad experience and not coming to terms with the bad experience, we form or create an energy blockage that could be carried from generation to generation in our basic blueprint.

Not until these blockages are dealt with at the root cause, they will continue to cause chronic pain with no known reason. As a healer, it is your job to find and remove these blockages. Wisdom is always in your questions.

Most people don't realize that personal poverty or homelessness is just as much a disease as the brand name diseases and can be healed just as effectively. In our society, it is one of the major diseases.

Healing personal poverty or homelessness and the feelings brought on by lack of adequate funds helps any of the brand name diseases.. Blessings to all who love and care for others.

What Is Curanderismo?

Curanderismo represents a holistic wellness approach with a longstanding history in the Americas, deeply rooted in ancient Native traditions spanning millennia. The effectiveness of this practice, which involves a comprehensive understanding of herb combinations, is acquired through the transmission of knowledge and hands-on experience. While not a lucrative field, those who choose a career in Curanderismo find fulfillment in aiding individuals who seek alternative healing methods.

The tradition of Curanderismo has been passed down through generations, and though initially tied to specific familial lineages, anyone can become a healer. In my practice, I integrate Reiki, enhancing healing effectiveness by 85%, coupled with the power of prayer and the assistance of celestial Reiki guides and angels. A recipient need not necessarily believe in the process but should be open to receiving prayers and the laying of hands.

I am enthusiastic about sharing my knowledge, offering teachings in Curanderismo, Reiki certifications (levels one to three), and Master Reiki Teacher certifications for those inclined to teach. I welcome anyone eager to learn these ritualistic healings, a tradition inherited from our ancestors.

Curanderas and Curanderos, practitioners of Curanderismo, are accessible to those seeking their services, typically providing reasonable fees. Some practitioners incorporate Tarot card readings into their services, combining spiritual guides, Reiki guides, and the pendulum for readings.

While I strive for accuracy in my readings, acknowledging that only God is infallible, I emphasize the importance of prayer to God or Mother God Anza. In my spiritual practice, I connect with guides from my past lives, anticipating that this is my final life on Earth. My Reiki Master has conveyed that the decision to return or not is mine, suggesting a possible return as a guide due to a familial need.

Reflecting on the challenges of guiding others, I question the effectiveness of being a voice in people's heads. Additionally, spiritual discernment is crucial to differentiate between positive spirits and potential psychic attacks. Personal experiences highlight the importance of safeguarding one's crown chakra and exercising caution with substances like alcohol and marijuana.

One specific healing technique within Curanderismo, known as "La barrida" or sweeping of the aura, involves using a straw broom with a wooden handle. This method, taught to me by my mother, is employed when individuals exhibit signs of negative attachments or entities affecting their behavior, health, or emotional well-being.

Thank you for considering these insights into the rich tradition of Curanderismo and its integration with other holistic healing practices.

La Barrida

To perform the traditional ritual of the barrida, gather the following items:

- A wooden broom handle with straw bristles
- A white clean sheet (wash separately after use)
- Candles
- A glass of water

Prioritize your protection with the Divine white light. Employ sacred symbols, such as those learned in Reiki, for added protection. Offer prayers to your highest source for protection and assistance.

Direct the person to lie on their back at the entrance of a doorway. Completely cover their body with the white sheet, securing it under the body. Position candles at the four corners of the body, corresponding to the North, East, South, and West.

On the glass of water, place the Sacred 4 Reiki symbols. Pray and hold the glass, activating it to cleanse the negative energy, pain, or entities surrounding the aura and body.

Take a mouthful of the blessed water, ensuring not to swallow it immediately. While holding the water, mentally petition the Divine Creator, your Guides, your Angels, the client's guides and angels, and the Arch-Angels (Rafael, Gabriel, and Miguel) for healing and protection. Request the expulsion of negative energy, bad luck, demons, illness, entities, and any unneeded spirits.

If the water is accidentally swallowed, take another mouthful from the same blessed glass.

Apply the Sacred 4 Reiki symbols to the broom. Pray and hold the broom, activating it to clear out negative energy, pain, or entities around the aura and body.

Begin sweeping above the body with the broom, ensuring not to touch the body. Start from the head, moving down to the feet and around the body, always sweeping in the direction towards the open door leading to the outside world. Trust that the Divine sources will handle the direction of negative energy, demons, or entities.

Standing on the side of the person, spray the water from your mouth from the head to the toes. If guided, repeat the water spray using the same water from the glass.

This concludes the traditional ritual of the barrida, known for its healing effects. Many individuals earnestly request this ritual, experiencing a notable difference in their energy afterward.

Additionally, consider the Limpiada de huevo cleansing, a practice involving the use of an egg to address ailments such as headaches, stomach aches, cramps, entity removal, and the elimination of the "evil eye" or negative energy. Administering this healing modality involves rubbing the egg over a person's body and has been known to provide relief for various afflictions..

Limpiada de huevo cleansing with an egg

This ancient healing method involving the use of an egg has its roots in various countries, and the Mexican tradition has preserved and passed down this practice from generation to generation, even in the modern era. Employing this technique has proven effective across a spectrum of illnesses, particularly with babies who are often given "el mal de Ojo" and are rubbed with an egg to ward off nightmares, ensuring restful sleep.

During my grandson's graduation party, despite the jubilant atmosphere, he suddenly experienced vomiting and complained of a severe headache. Amidst the festivities, I discreetly took him aside, performed the egg sweeping, and advised him to rest for a brief period. Remarkably, within approximately 10 minutes, he resumed socializing with his characteristic exuberance.

Perceiving the egg as a metaphorical magnet for drawing out negative energy, I have encountered skeptics who may question holistic healing in comparison to conventional medicine. Nevertheless, my personal experiences attest to the efficacy of using the egg, producing what might be considered miraculous results.

Instances abound where family members, previously ailing for weeks or months, made remarkable recoveries after undergoing the egg healing ritual. I have been both a witness and a practitioner of this method, fostering wellness in those who embraced this alternative approach.

For those inclined to use the egg for self-healing, the process involves:

1. Praying over the egg or making the sign of the cross three times.
2. Having a clear glass of water ready to break the egg into.
3. For Reiki practitioners, placing sacred symbols on the egg and requesting its activation.
4. Rubbing the egg in a clockwise motion on specific areas, including the head, eyes, ears, lips, neck, spine, arms, torso, and legs.
5. Holding the egg in your hands.
6. Placing it on the first chakra (between the thighs).
7. Breaking the egg into the glass, sprinkling salt on it.
8. After expressing gratitude to the egg, disposing of it by flushing it down the toilet or returning it to the earth through burial.

In a personal incident during my retirement party, where I fell ill despite the festivities, a curandero, my brother, performed the egg sweeping, enabling me to rejoin the celebration within 20 to 30 minutes after a brief respite. This method has proven effective in diverse situations, from dispelling negativity and bad luck to facilitating recovery from emotional and physical trauma.

While acknowledging my Catholic upbringing and baptism, the holistic healing practices rooted in religious beliefs are an integral part of our cultural heritage. Beginning the egg healing with the sign of the cross and prayers reflects the influence of these beliefs, reinforcing my unwavering faith in this age-old practice.

Why do Healers Become Ill?

The phenomenon of healers experiencing illness is indeed a fascinating topic that warrants consideration. Drawing from personal experiences and insights gleaned from Diane Stien's book, "What You Put Out Comes Back to You," I encountered a situation that underscored the reciprocity of energies in the universe.

Upon learning that a student had abruptly abandoned my daughter, leaving her to bear the financial burden of their shared apartment, I, in a fit of anger, inadvertently expressed a negative sentiment towards the student. Subsequently, I found myself grappling with unforeseen financial challenges. This served as a poignant lesson, a reminder from my guides about the interconnectedness of intentions and consequences.

As healers, it is crucial to recognize that the energy we emit into the universe has a reciprocal nature. Uttering careless words or harboring negative thoughts can create energetic leaks, attachments, and blockages. This accumulation of negativity may manifest in burnout, or in more severe cases, physical or emotional illness. In essence, the energy we project can influence the situations we encounter.

Reflecting on another incident involving a confrontational encounter on the road, where frustration led me to make a negative statement, I quickly realized the potential consequences of my words. Through an understanding and compassionate shift in perspective, I diffused the situation, emphasizing the importance of self-awareness and responsible energy management.

Healers, functioning as lightworkers, need to be especially cautious about harboring ill intentions towards others. The Ho'oponopono practice is highlighted as a method to rectify energetic imbalances and maintain harmony. Continual negativity, if left unchecked, may lead to burnout or a cascade of undesirable events.

Acknowledging our humanity, healers should actively seek guidance from their spiritual sources when confronted with challenging emotions. This proactive approach, combined with self-awareness, prevents unintentional negative energy release. As Abraham Hicks aptly notes, "you have 17 seconds to take things back," underscoring the importance of swift correction to avoid the unintended repercussions of negative energy manifestation.

2 UNUSUAL EMOTIONAL ISSUES

Individuals seeking Curandero Therapy often grapple with a spectrum of challenges deeply rooted in emotional and social histories extending over centuries.

These clients endeavor to navigate a new societal landscape that can prove challenging to assimilate, fostering sentiments of alienation, outcast status, or a perception of being relegated to a subordinate role within society. Providing compassionate support becomes instrumental in fostering a sense of belonging and empowerment, aiding these individuals in becoming valued contributors to the broader community.

The multifaceted nature of their issues manifests in diverse forms, with obesity frequently emerging as an outward expression of underlying concerns. Within the realm of Curandero Therapy, practitioners frequently find themselves assisting clients in addressing weight-related issues, recognizing that these concerns often serve as manifestations of deeper emotional and social complexities, common among many Americans.

Curandero Healing & Weight Loss

Let us initiate this process by invoking the sacred symbols of Reiki and seeking the guidance and assistance of our guides, angels, and any ascended masters in whom you place your belief. As we embark on this new endeavor, it is crucial to harness the strength and willpower required for its pursuit.

The question arises: Can Curanderismo be effectively employed for both healing and weight loss? Weight-related challenges have become increasingly prevalent, prompting reflection on the factors contributing to this issue.

Exploring the roots of weight gain necessitates an examination of various elements, such as dietary habits, portion sizes, and lifestyle choices.

For many, shedding excess weight is more straightforward during youth, typically requiring only modest physical activity. However, contemporary trends, where indoor activities, computer games, and electronic devices dominate recreation, pose obstacles to maintaining an active lifestyle. The prevalence of smartphones and computer-centric routines, exacerbated by pandemic-related restrictions, has shifted the paradigm, making it more challenging to engage in traditional forms of exercise like going to the gym.

The convenience of online grocery shopping, which allows for home delivery, has further facilitated a sedentary lifestyle. While this is advantageous for individuals with busy schedules or those who prefer limited social interactions, it underscores the importance of finding alternative means of physical activity.

Considering the potential consequences of prolonged inactivity, it is essential to acknowledge the critical role that movement plays in maintaining overall health. A poignant example underscores this point: a tragic incident involving an individual who, due to a sedentary routine, developed a blood clot that ultimately proved fatal. This serves as a stark reminder of the importance of incorporating regular movement into our daily lives, particularly when engaged in prolonged periods of computer use.

In conclusion, our bodies demand movement for optimal well-being, and as we navigate the prevalent use of computers and technology, incorporating regular exercise becomes imperative for maintaining a healthy and balanced lifestyle.

An Easy Way to Fix Your Health

Initiate your journey to self-improvement by cultivating a sense of self-love and practicing kindness when you gaze upon your reflection. Begin the process of self-appreciation with a focus on small, meaningful changes that collectively contribute to a significant transformation.

Our starting point involves a thoughtful examination of portion sizes, recognizing their pivotal role in achieving dietary balance. Rather than adopting extreme measures, such as eliminating entire food groups, we advocate for a sensible approach that avoids the pitfalls associated with such drastic actions. The misguided elimination of carbohydrates or fats can have adverse effects, impacting testosterone levels, energy, brain function, and nutrient absorption.

Avoiding overly processed empty calories, particularly simple carbohydrates that cause blood sugar spikes and subsequent crashes, is pivotal to dietary success. Examples of such foods include chocolates (except for dark chocolate), French fries, hamburgers, cakes, chips, white bread, candies, and soda drinks. Replace sugary beverages with ample amounts of refreshing water or infuse it with lime, lemon, or your preferred fruit for added flavor.

By eliminating processed foods, a substantial reduction in calorie intake is achieved. To enhance this effect, we propose a stricter dietary regimen, focusing specifically on the first two meals of the day. This approach aims to instill discipline and structure into your dietary habits.

Augmenting these efforts, harness the power of prayer and meditation to fortify your resolve and sustain the effectiveness of this transformative method. Engage in curandero practices, directing prayers towards the food you consume, beseeching that it nourishes your body with essential nutrients while expelling unwanted fats and calories.

Express gratitude for your body through the powerful practice of Ho'oponopono, emphasizing self-love and appreciation. In moments of temptation, exhibit strength by savoring a single bite of indulgence, demonstrating your ability to resist further consumption.

Leverage your spiritual resources, including angels, guides, Mother Azna, Ascending Masters, and Archangels such as Rafael, Michael, and Gabriel. Tap into these sources of support, as they stand ready to assist you on your journey of self-improvement and holistic well-being.

Can You Take Compliments?

How do you typically respond to compliments? Can you easily accept praise, or does it make you feel uneasy? The dynamics of receiving compliments and responding to them can be intricate and reveal a lot about our perception of ourselves.

It's intriguing how, in contrast to compliments, negative comments from strangers can be hurtful. Instances of unwarranted name-calling, such as being called the derogatory term "Bitch," can be disconcerting, particularly in bustling urban environments. While such encounters are often best left unaddressed, there might be occasions when understanding the source of conflict becomes necessary.

Reflecting on the impact of mean-spirited comments prompts consideration of our own reactions when subjected to criticism. Responding to criticism requires finesse, as it directly challenges one's sense of self. Counter-criticism may seem like a natural response, but it tends to exacerbate the situation, adding complexity to the interpersonal dynamic.

Paradoxically, when faced with kindness and positive remarks, many individuals find it challenging to accept the praise graciously. A common response involves downplaying one's achievements or deflecting compliments by highlighting perceived flaws. This inclination to reject compliments often stems from societal pressures discouraging self-praise, perceived as conceit or arrogance.

Cultural upbringing and teachings from parents or religious institutions contribute to this hesitancy to acknowledge one's accomplishments. The reluctance to embrace compliments may be rooted in a desire to avoid appearing boastful or self-centered.

A healthier approach to compliments involves a simple acknowledgment and expression of gratitude. Responding with a sincere "thank you" or "thank you very much" suffices, without the need to undermine one's accomplishments. It's crucial to recognize that accepting compliments doesn't equate to arrogance but rather demonstrates an appreciation for positive recognition.

Moreover, the cultural significance of gift-giving is highlighted, emphasizing the importance of accepting gifts graciously. Rejecting a gift can unintentionally convey a message of ingratitude, causing hurt to the giver. Cultural nuances dictate the value placed on giving the best one has, even if it entails personal sacrifice.

In conclusion, navigating compliments and criticisms requires a delicate balance. Embracing compliments with gratitude and accepting gifts with appreciation fosters positive interactions, while responding to negativity with resilience and understanding helps maintain emotional equilibrium. Being mindful of cultural sensitivities and societal expectations contributes to creating harmonious interpersonal connections.

Energy Vampires

Energy vampires are individuals who, at times intentionally, deplete your emotional energy by capitalizing on your willingness to listen and care for them. They often leave you feeling fatigued and overwhelmed.

These individuals possess a belief that others will provide them with attention when they are low on their own energy. Seeking solace in conversation, they expect you to make them feel better about themselves. Once the interaction concludes, they express gratitude for your attention and acknowledge your busy schedule before releasing you.

If you find that people frequently turn to you for conversation, exercise caution, as you may be a preferred outlet for those seeking understanding and compassion. People with good listening skills and a compassionate nature often become magnets for such individuals who can sense these qualities.

Sensitive individuals are particularly susceptible to energy vampires. Their offering of a listening ear, a kind heart, and boundless energy makes them prime targets for emotional drainage. In some instances, energy vampires exploit your innate qualities to drain you of your vital energy.

Energy vampires are adept at monopolizing your time during social occasions to extract as much of your energy as possible. They may consistently request coffee or dinner dates, knowing that you may feel guilty declining. Persistence in their requests may lead you to reluctantly agree, as they are keen on securing your time and attention.

Some energy vampires go to great lengths, even treating you to dinner at your favorite restaurant, to prolong conversations until exhaustion. If resistance is met, they may use various tactics, such as appealing to your favorite places or offering to cover expenses.

In situations where you reluctantly agree to lend them your energy, it is advisable to surround yourself with white light, a protective measure to expedite the process. Additionally, you can invoke your guides to connect with the guides of the energy vampire, facilitating an open reception to suggestions and, ideally, prompting them to conclude the interaction.

In instances where you find it necessary to cut short an interaction, it is acceptable to express prior commitments or the need to meet someone else. Maintaining politeness, you can assure them that you will reach out later. For those who persistently seek your energy, conveying that you will send positive energy their way can provide an alternative without compromising your well-being.

Dealing with such situations requires a delicate balance of setting boundaries, expressing care, and protecting your own energy.

Stressed about something?

Why do we subject ourselves to excessive stress? Stress seems to be a constant presence in our lives, leading to the question of whether we are inadvertently addicted to it. It's crucial to recognize that all pressure is ultimately self-imposed. While the originator of this idea escapes my memory, the concept suggests that stress, in essence, is a choice we make, even when external factors may make it feel imposed upon us.

Despite external influences, we possess the will to assert ourselves and declare that we won't allow bills, people, or our jobs to force us into a state of stress against our wishes. We maintain the ability to say "no" to stress, regardless of the potential consequences tied to the decisions we make.

Our control over our daily lives exceeds our awareness, perhaps because we seldom test the power of wishful thinking. Setting intentions upon waking is a practice I have found valuable. Deciding the kind of day we want to have, from the moment we start making morning coffee, allows us to establish a positive mindset. For instance, encountering an early mishap, like spilling coffee grounds, offers an opportunity to react with a smile and declare, "Today is going to be a wonderful morning." Incorporating gratitude, even for a single thing, can significantly alter the trajectory of the day.

In the workplace, faced with mounting tasks and paperwork, we often succumb to stress. Yet, instead of allowing anxiety to take hold, we can request assistance from our guides, angels, and the universe. By seeking help to manage phone calls and complete tasks, we create a pathway for a more productive day. The key is to simply ask.

Recognizing that all stress is self-imposed reinforces the idea that we have the power to choose how our day unfolds. This realization liberates us from the feeling of being a captive to stress, offering a fresh perspective on managing our lives.

If something in your life is causing physical or emotional distress, it's essential to identify and address the root cause. Stress at home or work can manifest in detrimental consequences. Taking a moment to reflect in front of the mirror can reveal the toll stress is taking on your well-being. Listen to your body, acknowledge the signs such as wrinkles and stomachaches, and consider whether it's time to change your situation, whether at work or home.

Seeking spiritual guidance, praying, and opening yourself to assistance from spiritual beings like Mother Azna can be instrumental in finding a path forward. Remember, you don't have to endure this state of stress indefinitely; you have the power to make a choice and explore alternative paths to a healthier, more balanced life.

Healing Relationships

How would you go about healing a strained relationship, whether it be with a family member, parents, or another family? There are instances where our words may have unintentionally hurt someone, and in hindsight, we realize the impact of our statements. Promptly apologizing may not always be the best course, as it could potentially exacerbate the situation.

A sincere apology, coupled with a physical gesture such as reaching out to touch their hand or arm, can convey authenticity. Expressing sentiments like, "I value our friendship and did not intend to cause harm; I am genuinely sorry," can aid in the healing process. While the other person may not immediately respond or engage, extending a heartfelt apology allows them the agency to decide the next steps.

Consider reversing the scenario – wouldn't you appreciate receiving a sincere apology? While initial hurt may linger, time often allows for the softening of emotions and a willingness to accept an apology. Recognize that it takes courage to apologize, and an even greater strength to accept one.

Ego and pride can often obstruct the path to resolution. Reflecting on past experiences may reveal instances where pride hindered the opportunity for reconciliation. Acknowledge the potential regret of not apologizing or accepting an apology in a timely manner.

If ongoing interaction with the person is necessary, consider engaging their Angels or guides, urging them to foster understanding and mend the relationship. Seek guidance from your own spiritual guides, asking for assistance in doing what is right. You may sense an internal push towards sincere actions that transcend notions of right or wrong when genuine love is at the core.

Should unease persist, envelop both yourself and the other person in a white divine light and engage in a calm, soft-spoken conversation. Emphasize the importance of fostering a positive relationship without harboring resentment. If the relationship is that of friends, consider offering a small token of appreciation, symbolizing your connection.

Implementing Reiki symbols can be a surprising yet effective approach. Visualize the symbols, particularly using Cho-Ku-Rei to activate the power of love and peace within yourself and the other person. The transformative effect of these practices may contribute to a sense of relief and positive change in the dynamics of the relationship.

Do You Believe in Curses?

Do you believe in the concept of curses? There have been instances, such as a woman arguing on Judge Judy that someone placed a curse on her, seeking compensation from the plaintiff. While this may seem peculiar, it underscores the seriousness with which some individuals approach the belief in curses. For those who genuinely hold such beliefs, the impact can be profound, leading them to seek the services of practitioners like Curanderas(os), Shamans, or witch doctors for curse removal.

The essence of a curse often lies in the belief placed in it. An illustrative example is the widely held belief in the curse associated with the unearthing of Tutankhamun's tomb. Media coverage of the excavation linked subsequent deaths and misfortunes within the archaeological team to a supposed curse. This phenomenon is sometimes labeled as magical thinking in psychological terms, indicative of a mental health symptom.

Cultural perspectives vary, with certain communities strongly embracing the potency of curses. The concept of curses can manifest in various forms, such as chain letters that threaten misfortune if not shared. Psychologists classify this as a self-fulfilling prophecy, akin to the idea of the law of attraction – a concept psychologists may acknowledge but struggle to explain scientifically.

In my cultural context as a Curandero/a Therapist, curses like the "evil eye" are addressed. The evil eye, a curse often associated with envy and jealousy, is believed to unravel the recipient's good fortune. While there is no scientific evidence supporting the supernatural basis of curses, psychologists attribute their impact to a person's self-confidence and well-being, often framing it within the context of mental health.

The exploration extends to the realm of spirits and supernatural occurrences, such as goosebumps or unexplained phenomena. While science may not provide definitive explanations for these experiences, many individuals claim various gifts or talents, such as seeing auras or visions of the future. The idea that we are not alone in the world, with extraterrestrial beings potentially aiding us, is also part of the supernatural narrative. Amid these uncertainties, the practice of enveloping oneself in Divine white light serves as a protective measure, reinforcing a sense of security when facing the unknown.

How to Get Rid of Unwanted Entities

Entities are non-physical energies or beings caught in dimensions where they may require assistance in transitioning. They can actively interfere with an individual's energy, emotions, and even occupy physical spaces like homes or rooms. While there is some acknowledgment of these phenomena, they are often misunderstood, and many lack the knowledge of how to address such beliefs. Certain indicators may suggest the presence of entities. It is recommended to surround oneself with Divine white light for protection before engaging with paranormal phenomena.

INDICATORS INCLUDE:

Unexplained drafts in areas with no apparent source.
Audible noises like conversations or footsteps when alone.
Lights flickering or bulbs suddenly burning out.
Persistent fatigue or feelings of extreme tiredness.
Sensation of being watched.
Spooky or unsettling feelings.
Depressive emotions within the home, alleviated when outside.
Intuitive sense that something is amiss.
Goosebumps when feeling observed.

WHAT TO DO:

In such cases, initiate a thorough smudging of the house using sage or a blend of sage and cedar incense. Allow the smoke to fill each room while praying for clearance in each corner, behind doors, and over windows. Communicate with the entity compassionately, expressing the intention to help them move on and alleviating any fear they may have.

At this point, you may feel the entity's presence. Send love and invite their spirit guides, urging them to guide the entity to their rightful place. Approach with gentleness and politeness, as even in their non-physical state, they can still perceive threat.

If the entity refuses or expresses uncertainty, assure them of your benevolent intentions. Spirits may be hesitant due to uncertainty or fear, and they may require assurance from familiar figures like relatives or past pets. Request that their spirit guides bring forth someone familiar to guide them home.

To confirm the entity's attachment, use a pendulum, observing its clockwise swing. Once convinced, request that they release their energy from the pendulum after crossing over, indicated by a slowdown or stoppage. The theory surrounding spirit attachments suggests that they complete a pre-agreed learning experience, and once this is accomplished, they are ready to move on.

Spirit attachments, encountered during healing, indicate a readiness for transition. These entities, stuck in lower-dimensional realms, do not belong there. The release during healing benefits both the person and the healer.

After healing entities, it is crucial to smudge or sage the area for complete clearance. Leaving residue could potentially cause health issues such as headaches or diarrhea. Always ensure personal protection by surrounding yourself with Divine white light when dealing with entities.

Psychic Attacks and Marijuana

What is the correlation between psychic attacks and marijuana? Although marijuana is often perceived as a benign substance, its effects on consciousness can lead to altered states. Some individuals incorporate it into their daily routines, using it before, during, or after work, seeking the euphoric high it provides for a few hours. While marijuana has proven beneficial for certain medical conditions and anxiety issues, its recreational use solely for the purpose of intoxication raises questions about its impact on spiritual well-being.

Some practitioners, including healers, employ marijuana to facilitate connections with spirits. They may seek assistance from specific entities for various purposes, such as addressing curses or illnesses. However, this practice raises concerns about its ethical and spiritual implications. Certain spirits, akin to genies, may offer assistance but often require something in return, potentially leading to complications.

Extended use of marijuana without a clear intention or purpose may result in unforeseen consequences. Over time, individuals may notice negative shifts in their experiences, such as a string of bad luck, vehicular breakdowns, and a series of minor misfortunes. These occurrences may be attributed to the altered state induced by consistent marijuana use.

In particular, there is a spiritual concern associated with the open-ended use of marijuana. Smoking marijuana has been linked to the attraction of entities, including earthbound spirits—individuals who may not realize they have passed away and remain bound to the earthly plane. The prolonged use of marijuana leaves the 7th crown chakra, the energy-receiving point from the divine (Source, God, the universe), vulnerable and open. This vulnerability allows entities, and potentially demons, to attach themselves to an individual's energy or aura.

While marijuana is not comparable to highly addictive and destructive substances like heroin or crack, it is considered a slow and subtle killer. It may serve as a gateway drug, leading individuals to seek more intense experiences. Observational data suggests that a significant portion of individuals struggling with addiction started with marijuana as their initial drug of choice.

To protect oneself from potential negative spiritual influences associated with marijuana use, it is advised to reconsider engaging in the recreational or habitual consumption of this substance. The susceptibility to entities and demons that may be attracted during marijuana use poses potential risks to spiritual and mental well-being. It is essential to weigh the potential consequences and make informed decisions regarding substance use, especially for those who hold spiritual beliefs.

Soldier Haunted by K.I.A.

During a session with a former Soldier, who was referred by another client and visiting from another country, he shared a recurring issue of stomach pain after dinner since arriving in the United States. Attributing it to a possible disagreement with the local food, he stayed with a family from his hometown who were temporarily in the U.S. for the cherry-picking season.

To address his discomfort, I applied an ancient remedy passed down from my mother. The remedy involved placing a dishtowel containing a cut onion and three scrambled eggs on his stomach or belly button area for 15 to 20 minutes, using the warmth of the towel to draw out any negative energy or illness. I also advised him not to consume any liquids during his meal.

Upon his return the following week, he reported relief for a few days, but the pain resurfaced. Employing my pendulum, I assessed his chakras and detected a heaviness on the left side of his body, indicating an attachment. Taking necessary precautions, I sought guidance from my angels, his angels, and my guides to understand the situation.

Facing difficulty in discerning the issue, I enlisted the help of my psychic reading friends. Through their connections with angels and guides, I received images and sensations, visualizing a man in uniform (the client) holding someone who had died in his arms. The client confirmed that he had experienced such an incident during the war in El Salvador, where a friend had died in his arms after being shot in the stomach.

In collaboration with the client, I sought permission to spiritually guide his friend back home. Utilizing my pendulum, I requested the friend's energy to detach from the client's body. As the pendulum circled clockwise, I conveyed the message of spiritual freedom through belief in Jesus, emphasizing his release from sins. The pendulum halted, signifying the friend's successful transition.

Later that night, the client reported relief from stomach pain, even after consuming fluids during dinner. He expressed gratitude on Sunday, bringing a gift of freshly picked Bing cherries. His pain had disappeared, and he attributed it to the spiritual release facilitated during the session.

Shifting our Mood Along with Earth

Navigating through life with a positive attitude can indeed be challenging, yet the process of shifting one's mood is not as formidable as it may seem. Especially during moments of sadness, depression, or negativity, the practice of gratitude can serve as a transformative tool.

There are times when the buoyancy of perpetually optimistic individuals can be irksome. When confronted with such scenarios, where exuberant colleagues or acquaintances seem unaffected by gloom, a natural aversion may arise. However, a realization struck me during a conversation with a consistently cheerful coworker. Inquiring about the source of her perpetual good mood, she attributed it to gratitude for her job, each day bestowed upon her by a higher power, and the opportunity to assist others within our Mental Health agency.

Reflecting on this perspective, I recognized the importance of cultivating gratitude in my own life. Acknowledging my ability to communicate with guides, provide energy clearings, and contribute to healing processes, I found ample reasons for gratitude. In the context of the ongoing global challenges, being untouched by the prevailing virus further intensified my sense of appreciation.

The Earth's gradual shift, observable since the turn of the millennium, elicits gratitude for the measured pace of change. This deliberate transformation impacts various facets of our existence, from government structures and telecommunication systems to energy sources and dietary habits. This shift also enhances our intuitive capacities and elevates our frequency, akin to animals sensing impending earthquakes.

As we collectively evolve, embracing a happier and more fulfilling existence becomes paramount. Understanding the nuances of the spiritual realm and heeding the guidance of angels, our higher selves, and spiritual beings, we embark on a journey of self-discovery. The whispers of our higher selves, reminiscent of our own voice but imbued with wisdom, encourage attentive listening.

Amidst the global shifts, there is an inherent readiness for change that prepares us for the evolving landscape. Fostering a sense of gratitude for the support and guidance offered by spiritual beings becomes instrumental in elevating our frequency. As we attune ourselves to this changing world, our spiritual companions celebrate our moments of happiness, joy, and peace.

Expressing gratitude for their guidance, we align our frequency with a positive trajectory, navigating life with a profound sense of appreciation during this transformative period.

Our Spiritual Career Paths

Have you considered integrating your spiritual guides into your career trajectory? The quest for an ideal career often leads us to contemplate the intersection of passion and financial stability. Contrary to conventional wisdom, achieving both is not an insurmountable feat, especially for individuals with a spiritual inclination. The universe responds to those who project their energy into it, and articulating specific career aspirations can be a powerful catalyst for manifestation.

Engage in thorough research to discern the type of job or career that resonates with your professional goals and personal fulfillment. Rather than a generic wish for a good-paying job, employ meditation or prayer to articulate your desires with precision. Specify the nature of the job, envisaging an environment surrounded by positive colleagues, where your contributions are valued and where you derive a sense of fulfillment. Open-mindedness is key in this process.

For those who believe in their spiritual guides and angels, involving them in this journey is highly encouraged. Consider the notion that God, angels, and guides were instrumental in initiating your career path before your incarnation, aligning it with your interests and purpose. A compelling example is a client who, from a young age, exhibited a penchant for building things. Guided by his passion, he now successfully buys and sells houses.

Seek divine assistance in your educational pursuits as well. A client, who fervently requested God's guidance, received financial support and successfully pursued education in his chosen field. Clients often approach me seeking guidance on finding the right job. In such instances, I prompt them to introspect about their passions and, when necessary, invoke the assistance of their angels and guides.

Remarkably, some have ventured into entrepreneurship, establishing prosperous businesses. Others have secured fulfilling employment within their state, forming meaningful connections and enjoying lucrative careers. For those with a spiritual calling to contribute positively to the world, such endeavors can manifest in various forms, including activism aimed at preserving the environment.

Consider individuals protesting deforestation, driven by a desire to mitigate the adverse effects of pollutants on the earth. Those attuned to the guidance of their angels and guides are already fulfilling their destinies and earth purposes. Reflect on your own purpose and how you can contribute to the betterment of others. If assisting others resonates with you, explore career paths such as aiding in tax preparation, supporting low-income families, or working in healthcare.

Pondering your purpose may yield multiple interests. In such cases, be open to trying different paths. The gentle voice guiding you may not always be immediately recognizable, so maintain openness and patience in the process. Allow your divine angels to illuminate the way as you embark on a journey toward a fulfilling and purposeful career.

3 POWERFUL PERCEPTIONS

Do You Believe in Superstition?

A percentage of the global population adheres to superstitions. Superstition, lacking a singular definition, generally refers to a belief in supernatural forces, such as fate, a desire to influence unpredictable factors, and a need to address uncertainty. People often utter phrases like "Bless you" or "Salud" (meaning health) when someone sneezes, as a precaution against potential bad luck. The act of "knocking on wood" is another common superstition, attributing one's well-being to this ritual.

Carrying items for good luck, like a rabbit's foot, raises questions about the origin of such beliefs. The avoidance of the number 13 in hotels and motels is a well-known superstition, with variations like the avoidance of the number 17 in Italy and Brazil.

Psychologists posit that superstitions may stem from an assumed connection between events and unrelated occurrences. Examples include the belief that walking under a ladder brings bad luck or that encountering a black cat, especially one crossing the path, foretells an accident. Engaging in superstitions often provides individuals with a perceived sense of control and helps alleviate anxiety during stressful situations.

Common superstitions include not walking on sidewalk cracks to avoid causing harm to one's mother, covering mirrors when someone dies, and refraining from placing two mirrors facing each other due to an association with the devil. Other superstitions advise against heading straight home after a funeral to prevent attaching spirits to oneself, toasting with water in German tradition to avert potential death, and interpreting itches on specific palms as omens for financial gain or loss.

Further superstitions caution against placing a bed on the north side of the bedroom due to bad energy, associating the presence of an owl in one's home with a foreboding omen of death, and trying on a bride's wedding ring as a harbinger of future marriage troubles. Breaking mirrors is considered a source of seven years of bad luck, and opening umbrellas inside a house is thought to invite misfortune.

While these superstitions may sound peculiar, it's crucial to respect individuals' beliefs, as some take them seriously. Adhering to such practices may seem like playing it safe, acknowledging the uncertainty that surrounds superstitions. Additionally, placing the divine white light upon oneself is often recommended for protection.

What Are Good Luck Charms?

What constitutes lucky charms, and do they hold genuine efficacy? This question has been frequently posed by my clients, with some expressing the desire for me to activate objects they believe carry luck. The concept of luck is fundamentally tied to one's state of mind. Numerous studies have revealed a correlation between a positive attitude and a sense of good luck, suggesting that individuals with optimistic perspectives tend to experience greater satisfaction in various aspects of their lives.

The effectiveness of luck, as perceived through charms or activated objects, is contingent upon the energy invested in them. According to the principles of the law of attraction, channeling sufficient energy into a belief or object can potentially yield positive outcomes. In a previous chapter, I explored the activation of objects, a concept applicable to lucky charms. The belief in the influence of specific colors or outfits on one's sense of power, miracles, or wish fulfillment is grounded in the idea that these elements can enhance one's aura, instilling confidence and garnering the belief of others.

Certain items, colors, or outfits indeed have the capacity to evoke feelings of ambition, luck, or confidence. The impact of these feelings is largely dependent on how individuals elevate their mental and emotional states. Engaging in activities like research, cultivating curiosity, and fostering a positive interpretation of the world contribute to building a positive mindset, thereby attracting positive energy and, potentially, a streak of good luck.

The law of attraction posits that by fostering a positive outlook and aligning oneself with optimistic people, individuals can attract the luck they seek. Surrounding oneself with positive friends and family members who exude confidence and contribute to a positive environment can significantly influence one's attitude and overall sense of luck. Practicing patience is equally crucial, as success and happiness often unfold gradually.

Preparation and knowledge are paramount when facing challenges or opportunities. Acquiring the necessary knowledge, experience, and the ability to recognize and seize opportunities amidst the noise contribute to the formation of positive patterns. The courage to take chances is often misconstrued as luck but is, in reality, the result of informed decision-making and prudent choices.

Realistically and practically accomplishing personal goals involves maintaining a positive attitude and projecting it into the universe. Clearly defining one's desires and putting them forth to the universe aligns with the notion that what people perceive as luck is often the outcome of their own positive energy, attitude, and intentional choices.

Objects With Unusual Energy

Have you ever sensed peculiar energy emanating from objects, places, or encountered a distinct vibe from something you passed by? I recall an instance where I attended a garage sale and purchased a toilet paper holder shaped like a doll with a full skirt for a mere 2 dollars. It seemed cute, so I placed it on the toilet lid. However, each time I entered the bathroom, an inexplicable and eerie feeling accompanied it. The discomfort prompted me to part with the item, and the unsettling sensation dissipated. Has a similar occurrence transpired in your life?

In later years, I learned that many things carry unique energies, not necessarily negative, but some individuals, myself included, are particularly sensitive to specific energies. Analogously, when you become a parent, your heightened sense of smell enables you to discern scents more acutely. Similarly, with energy, familiarity with different types allows you to recognize when an unfamiliar energy is present.

Consider the connection you have with your vehicle; a new car may lack the inherent trustworthiness felt with an old car that reliably navigated you to your destinations. Cars, like old houses, possess energies that can be acknowledged and communicated with. Have you ever prayed or surrounded yourself with divine white light for protection before embarking on a trip, even a brief one to the store? If ensuring your safety is a priority, it is advisable.

My intriguing experiences extend to a new residence, an aged house where I perceived footsteps during both day and night. Cleaning the basement for my Reiki and Curandera consultation room, I sensed a constant presence, akin to conversations and movement. It turned out that three spirits were the guardians and custodians of the house, ensuring the exclusion of negative energies. In my consultation room, footsteps above indicated their protective vigilance.

Maintaining positive communication with these spirit protectors became a crucial aspect of my daily life. They would alert me if unfamiliar individuals were around the house at night, prompting me to illuminate all the lights. The bond was so profound that when I moved, I desired to take them with me, yet they conveyed their connection to the house and couldn't accompany me. Expressing gratitude for their guardianship, I revisited the house years later to find new occupants acknowledging similar experiences.

In contrast, newer houses lack such protectors, possibly due to their recent construction and the absence of accrued energies.

Has Anyone Explained Orbs?

The mystery of orbs captured in photographs has intrigued many, with explanations ranging from camera anomalies to paranormal manifestations. Some attribute these spherical anomalies to the camera lens or reflections from external light sources, resulting in circular artifacts caused by dust, water droplets, or other particles in the air or water. The scientific viewpoint, as articulated by Wikipedia, categorizes these phenomena as backscatter, common in modern digital cameras.

Despite scientific explanations, a multitude of individuals report experiencing a paranormal connection with orbs. Personal anecdotes, such as capturing orbs in times of emotional distress or spiritual significance, add layers of complexity to the phenomenon. One observer recounts photographing a distressed family member and consistently capturing orbs in the images.

Vanessa Williams, an energy worker and astrologer, offers a unique perspective on orbs. She views them as blessed manifestations representing spirits traversing through the camera lens. Williams believes that orbs serve as confirmations of guidance and protection by unseen energies. According to her, orbs symbolize the presence of the human soul, especially during moments when loved ones and ancestors seek to make themselves known through photographs and videos.

Another corroborating voice comes from Erica Davis, a lightworker who discovered her mediumistic abilities through orb encounters. Davis shares her initial fright at witnessing an orb with her naked eye, followed by subsequent appearances in security camera footage and personal family photos. Notably, she attests to seeing faces in these orbs, perceiving them as intelligent entities exhibiting purposeful movements. For Davis, these manifestations are indicative of souls seeking to communicate their presence.

The convergence of such diverse experiences prompts contemplation on the nature of orbs—spirits, loved ones, extraterrestrial entities, or enigmatic phenomena from alternate dimensions. While scientific interpretations remain rooted in optical explanations, the personal narratives of individuals like Vanessa Williams and Erica Davis contribute to the ongoing exploration of these mysterious occurrences, leaving the true nature of orbs open to interpretation and speculation. As we continue to unravel the mysteries around us, the veil between dimensions appears to lift, inviting us to pay attention to the unexplained and embrace the wonders of discovery.

How to Open the Third Eye

The concept of the "Third Eye" holds a mystique associated with heightened spiritual perception and cognitive clarity. Positioned between our physical eyes, this center is believed to facilitate a connection with the spirit world. When obstructed, it can contribute to mental fog, concentration issues, and decision-making challenges. Unblocking and healing the third eye involves holistic approaches, encompassing the healing of other Chakras and a mindful lifestyle.

Begin by assessing and healing your Chakras, utilizing techniques explained in previous chapters. This establishes a foundation for opening the third eye.

Engage in activities such as yoga, particularly Kundalini yoga, and maintain a nutritious diet. Nutritional wellness plays a crucial role in enhancing overall spiritual health.

Practice meditation with a focus on the third eye. If acquainted with Reiki symbols, incorporate Sei-He-Ki, Dai-ko-Myo, Cho-Ku-Rei, and Hon-Sha-Ze-Sho-Nen during meditation for long-distance healing.

Gently tap the third eye three times with each Reiki symbol or, if unfamiliar with the symbols, perform three taps directly on the third eye area.

Concentrate on the pineal and pituitary glands in the brain during meditation, envisioning the activation of these spiritual centers.

Hold a purple or amethyst crystal on the third eye, affirming, "It is okay for me to see." Repeat until any fear or tension dissipates.

Rotate the amethyst clockwise on the third eye while reiterating the affirmation.

Bathe the stone and your third eye in the Divine white light, invoking spiritual assistance from guides and angels for vision interpretation.

Take three deep breaths, holding the third breath for a mental count of 6, and exhale.

For those seeking clairvoyance or aiding others in the process, perform the exercises collaboratively. Overcoming fear is pivotal; request protection from guides, angels, or a higher source.

In instances of overwhelming visions, seek guidance on handling what is within your control. Establish boundaries, as personal visions can evoke powerful emotions and may extend beyond direct influence.

Maintain a dialogue with your guides, angels, or higher source, requesting visions aligned with your capacity to positively impact outcomes.

Remember to prioritize protection during these practices, enveloping yourself in the Divine white light. This comprehensive approach integrates spiritual, physical, and mental elements, fostering a balanced and harmonious connection with the third eye.

How to Contact Your Totem Animal

The presence of totem animals in our lives is not obligatory, yet they often manifest in various forms, whether real or mythical. Consider your surroundings – the figures, stuffed animals, and creatures that draw your interest. Is there a particular animal, real or fantastical, that captures your fascination? Identifying your totem animal involves introspection and connection with personal symbolism.

Begin by contemplating the animals that consistently pique your interest. Are there specific figures or stuffed animals in your vicinity that hold significance? Totem animals, akin to spirit guides, may evoke emotional responses. Reflect on how these animals make you feel and the thoughts they generate.

Discovering your totem animal involves a meditative or prayerful process. Envision a serene, grassy meadow reminiscent of scenes from "The Wizard of Oz." As you relax, allow your totem animal to materialize a few feet away, radiating a sense of safety and warmth.

Engage in a conversation with your totem animal, observing its form, color, and nuances. Delve into its thoughts and inquire about its past assistance in your life. Seek insights into how it can continue to support you in the future. Acknowledge its inherent power and request confirmation of its role as your totem animal.

As the meditation concludes, ask your totem animal to manifest in other aspects of your life – dreams, TV, magazines, or through external conversations. Embrace the idea that these encounters are not mere coincidences but deliberate affirmations of your totem animal's presence.

Conclude the meditation by stepping back into your physical self, reorienting through deep breaths, and returning to full awareness. Remember that your totem animal may extend beyond the confines of traditional fauna, encompassing mythological beings such as dragons or unicorns. Delve into research to understand the traits and symbolism associated with your totem animal, recognizing the boundless nature of spirit animals.

4 METAPHYSICAL INTEGRATIONS

Reiki, a practice that holds a significant place in my life as a Reiki Master and Teacher, encapsulates a profound realm of healing. Merging the magic of Reiki with my Curandera skills and prayers, I have witnessed its potent impact on healing. This ancient laying-on hands technique, dating back thousands of years, serves as a powerful conduit for channeling the Universal life force energy, fostering well-being.

Reiki, meaning the Universal of the soul, transcends traditional boundaries and flows through all living things. Originating as a Tibetan Buddhist practice, it resurfaced in the late 1800s through the rediscovery by Dr. Mikao Usui, a Japanese Buddhist. This potent healing energy can be harnessed for self-healing or extended to others, making it a versatile and accessible form of healing.

In my practice, I utilize Reiki to activate energy in water and vitamins, alleviating aches and pains. The sacred symbols of Reiki find their place in my sage, enhancing the energy when smudging my home and car – a practice infused with prayers for safety and abundance. This transformative energy extends to the activation of the "egg" for countering the "evil eye," amplifying its healing properties.

The synergy of Reiki with Curandera skills and sacred symbols multiplies the potency of intentions for goodness and blessings. It aligns with the belief that Reiki is the boundless energy of the universe, channeled through practitioners' hands to benefit recipients. This God-given power is ready to bestow healing upon those open to its touch.

A personal testament to the efficacy of Reiki unfolded when I faced a concerning health situation. With symptoms that raised cancer-related fears, I turned to Reiki symbols, the white light of the divine spirit, and continuous prayer. The weekend-long process culminated in a shower revelation on Monday morning – the inexplicable disappearance of the perceived lumps and beads.

Subsequent medical examinations, prompted by an unexpected hospital call, confirmed the absence of any anomalies. The profound impact of Reiki had averted a potential health crisis. Over two decades later, my belief in Reiki remains unwavering, marked by a lack of any breast-related issues.

Reiki, when embraced and integrated with sacred symbols, transcends the physical realm. Its magic, coupled with divine connection, extends its influence to seemingly limitless domains, offering solace and healing on every level.

Terrorized By an Entity

I am pleased to announce another Reiki retreat, inviting Reiki Masters, teachers, students, and Reiki enthusiasts to my residence for a comprehensive three-day event. This retreat will focus on imparting knowledge and hands-on practice of Reiki levels 1, 2, and 3, catering to those eager to delve into the transformative world of Reiki healing.

For those attending, I extend a special offer: each petitioner is encouraged to bring a friend, entitling the petitioner to attend for free. The nominal cost for each participant is $150. Additionally, attendees contributing by bringing a shared snack and assisting with breakfast will benefit from a $10 deduction.

Accommodations for those staying overnight include a comfortable bed and a wholesome breakfast served on Saturday and Sunday mornings. On Friday afternoon, early arrivals have the opportunity to choose their beds and, in some cases, their rooms.

Over the years, this retreat has been a source of joy and learning, attracting up to 32 participants to my 5-bedroom home. In the spirit of camaraderie, some attendees willingly opted for sleeping arrangements on the carpeted floors.

One remarkable episode from a past retreat involved a Reiki petitioner who brought his sister. She was grappling with drug addiction, earnestly seeking a way to overcome it. During our Friday evening gathering, which includes breathing exercises and a collective prayer or meditation, the sister chose not to participate, having only been invited as the petitioner's guest.

As the night unfolded, distressing screams pierced the silence, revealing the sister's profound turmoil. She was imploring her brother to take her home, convinced that she was in imminent danger. Her fear emanated from entities tormenting her.

Responding to the tumult, I approached her door with reassurance, mentally enveloping both of us in the divine white light. Calmly, I assured her of safety and my genuine intent to help. Engaging with my guides and angels, I aimed to establish a connection with her guides.

Her apprehension stemmed from entities afraid of losing their hold on her, preventing her detachment from substance abuse. In my mind's eye, I perceived a skeletal, malevolent entity with a desperate grip on her, fueling her addiction.

Through multiple sessions, we successfully cleared her of these attachments – a total of nine entities. Over time, she triumphed over her addiction, transforming into a close friend who now joins me in aiding others struggling with drug dependency.

This retreat not only serves as a platform for Reiki training but also fosters a supportive community where healing transcends the physical to address profound spiritual and emotional challenges.

Spiritual Tingling Means

Have you ever experienced a tingling sensation on the back of your neck, tingling or goosebumps on your arms, or an unexplained chill? While a physical chill may simply indicate coldness, the spiritual interpretation of these sensations holds deeper meaning related to your aura and the energy surrounding you.

Spiritual tingling sensations often signify a presence around you – perhaps a visitation from a friend, relative, or an earthbound spirit. These occurrences are considered signs from spirit guides and angels attempting to establish contact or create a connection with you.

Alternatively, these sensations may be a response to receiving much-needed answers to persistent questions or uncertainties in your life, be it related to a job, a relationship, or any matter you've been grappling with.

For those seeking insights, using a pendulum can be a valuable tool. Ensuring a connection with your angels and guides, you can tap into spiritual guidance and assistance.

It's crucial to recognize that you are an integral part of a universal plan, like a missing puzzle piece waiting to fall into place. The spiritual sensations you experience might be nudges from the universe, guiding you toward your next steps or encouraging you to move in the right direction.

Even if you don't immediately notice goosebumps, those who are attuned to their body and spiritual senses often find that such sensations coincide with finding answers or resolutions – whether it be related to a job, the right furniture, or any confusion you may have been facing.

Consider instances when you notice something out of the corner of your eye, experiencing a shadow, and getting a chill. While it might be tempting to dismiss it as imagination, such occurrences often serve as subtle reminders. It could be a recent departed loved one reaching out to assure you that they are okay and not to worry.

Interestingly, dogs, children, and some individuals with heightened sensitivity have the ability to perceive ghosts or entities. Children, in particular, may express fear or wake up crying, seeking comfort. If you encounter such situations, there are preventive measures, such as using a protective spray in children's rooms, to create an environment that deters unwanted entities.

Understanding and acknowledging these spiritual sensations can lead to a deeper connection with the metaphysical realm and offer insights into the guidance and support available from spiritual guides and angels.

For a potent spiritual cleansing spray, gather the following ingredients and tools:

- Three cups of rubbing alcohol.
- Two teaspoons of salt.
- A spray bottle.

If you are familiar with Reiki practices, enhance the mixture's energy by placing the Sei-He-Ki, Dai-Ko-Myo, Hen-She-Ze-Sho-Nen symbols, and activate them with Cho-Ku-Rei.

Combine the ingredients in the spray bottle. Hold the bottle in your hands, activating the mixture, and direct your prayers to the divine source or any higher power you connect with, seeking the elimination of all negativity and entities.

Spray the mixture around the room and within the aura surrounding the individual affected. This application effectively addresses various spiritual disturbances.

Alternatively, consider smudging the room with sage, as this method also proves effective.

When experiencing spiritual sensations, it is essential to approach them purposefully. Engage in prayer and envelop yourself in the protective white light of the divine source. This act doesn't necessitate a particular belief; simply perform it for added safeguarding. Remember, spiritual cleansing is a thoughtful practice, and its efficacy can be augmented by integrating these elements into your routine.

Are You Hearing Voices?

Have you ever experienced the sensation of hearing your name being called, only to find no one around? These occurrences, while initially unsettling, often carry spiritual significance. When voices or thoughts manifest as if calling your name, it could be a loved one conveying a message of reassurance about their well-being.

In the realm of spiritual connections, instances where thoughts materialize into phone calls from the person you were contemplating are not uncommon. These occurrences serve as a testament to the interconnected nature of our minds and the profound influence of thoughts and intentions.

In the morning, when your mind is fresh from sleep, you might distinctly hear a voice saying your name. Far from signaling any mental decline, this often indicates a greeting from your angels or guides. These divine entities may choose such moments as they align with our heightened receptivity to spiritual communication upon waking.

According to the wisdom shared by a Curandera, questioning one's sanity in such situations is a sign of sanity itself. Those attuned to spiritual energies often experience sensations like covers moving or beds gently shifting, accompanied by goosebumps. These occurrences signify visits from spiritual entities, perhaps conveying love and well-wishes.

The power of vibrations in spiritual connections cannot be understated. Strong vibrations occur when someone is thinking of you, creating a link that may manifest in various ways, such as receiving a call, email, or message from the person in question.

Asking questions in prayer or meditation can yield swift responses, sometimes embedded in song lyrics that resonate with your thoughts. Music, with its universal language, may serve as a conduit for divine messages.

When encountering mysterious voices, seeking clarification on the identity of the speaker is a practical step. Genuine entities will provide identifiers that evoke emotions or memories unique to them. Deceased loved ones may sound familiar, often with restored strength and vitality.

In navigating these spiritual experiences, always invoke the presence of your angels and guides for reassurance. Utilize the protective power of white light to foster a sense of security and guardianship. These practices ensure a grounded and protected exploration of the spiritual realm.

Ringing in Your Ears? What Does it Mean?

Experiencing intermittent ringing in the ears is a phenomenon familiar to many lightworkers. It's crucial to shed light on this occurrence, as it often serves as a mode of communication from spiritual entities. Contrary to misconceptions, one doesn't require extraordinary gifts to perceive these subtle messages.

Individuals encountering such instances might dismiss them as anomalies or attribute them to trivial factors like earaches or earwax. However, it's essential to consider the possibility that these sounds may be attempts by angels or guides from another dimension to convey a message, often resembling the chirping of birds or a high-pitched tone.

Discerning these messages involves paying attention to specific details. The ringing typically occurs in one ear, and practitioners attuned to spiritual energies often request clearer communication when experiencing these sensations. The faint voice accompanying the ringing is akin to a small entity attempting to capture one's attention. Observing tingles, vibrations, or goosebumps may provide additional context, indicating the message is tied to a question or prayer seeking resolution.

During readings or moments of spiritual connection, practitioners often receive visions or thoughts accompanied by overwhelming feelings of love, evoking tears. These instances represent communication from angels, guides, or other spiritual entities.

For example, a sudden high-pitched ringing in the right ear while lying in bed signifies a spiritual being attempting to relay a message through the crown chakra. At times, practitioners might hear white noise or a sudden loud ringing, prompting them to request clearer communication from their angels.

Instances where practitioners misinterpret these messages as mundane sounds, like a refrigerator noise or potential tinnitus, underscore the importance of recognizing and acknowledging spiritual communications. Adjusting perceptions and asking angels to communicate more clearly can reveal the intended message, ensuring practitioners do not dismiss profound spiritual interactions as mere auditory anomalies.

Angels, deceased loved ones, and archangels each have distinct frequencies in their communication. Angels communicate with Shakespearean eloquence, offering direct and concise messages. Deceased loved ones maintain the same familiar voice from their earthly existence, often using personal nicknames. Archangels, akin to the voice of God, project a loud, direct, yet profoundly loving and respectful communication.

Understanding these frequencies enhances practitioners' ability to discern and embrace spiritual messages, dispelling doubts and fostering a deeper connection with the divine. Clarifying these nuances in spiritual communication can transform dismissive reactions into receptive acknowledgment.

What is Claircognizance?

In the realm of psychic phenomena, individuals often experience unexplained insights or knowledge during classes or training sessions. This intuitive knowing is referred to as Claircognizance, one of several psychic abilities that individuals may possess. Let's delve into the distinct characteristics of Clairvoyance, Claircognizance, Clairaudience, and Clairsentience.

1. **Clairvoyance (Clear Seeing):**

   - Definition: Psychic seeing, often expressed through phrases like "I see."
   - Experience: Visions, images, colors, symbols, and mental videos manifest in the mind's eye.

2. **Claircognizance (Clear Knowing):**

   - Definition: The intuitive ability of clear knowing without a logical basis.
   - Experience: Repetitive and positive insights that provide guidance for personal and collective improvement.

3. **Clairaudience (Clear Hearing):**

   - Definition: Intuitive ability related to clear hearing.
   - Experience: Perceiving messages or guidance through clear auditory channels.

4. **Clairsentience (Clear Feeling):**

   - Definition: Loosely translated as "clear-feeling."
   - Experience: Sensing or feeling intuitive information, often related to emotions.

True Claircognizance serves as a valuable tool for locating misplaced items or addressing personal concerns. By seeking guidance from spirit guides or angels, individuals can receive sudden insights or visions. A practical example is the retrieval of lost car keys, where an individual, after invoking guidance, envisions the keys stored in a jacket.

The power of Claircognizance extends beyond personal matters to professional realms. Individuals possessing this ability can inspire and assist others effectively. This divine force, originating from the creator, aligns with one's true talents and passions, guiding individuals to leverage their skills for the betterment of others.

Claircognizance communicates through repetitive thoughts, feelings, visions, or words, offering step-by-step instructions. Divine transmissions occur during receptive moments such as dream time, meditation, exercise, or even when the mind is in a relaxed state, such as watching TV.

To strengthen the connection with this intuitive ability, trusting and following one's intuition becomes crucial. This trust enhances the alignment with the guidance system provided by angels or guides. By venturing forward with confidence, individuals tap into true Divine wisdom, witnessing the seamless alignment of circumstances.

Personal experiences with psychic abilities may vary, encompassing sight, feelings, knowledge, and auditory perceptions. Ancestral connections may manifest, with unique triggers such as water providing conduits for receiving messages. While experiences differ among individuals, the consistent thread lies in the ability to seek spiritual help by simply asking and being receptive to the guidance offered.

Out of Body Projection

An intriguing phenomenon that often sparks skepticism is the idea of out-of-body experiences. Sylvia Brown proposes the notion that our spirits temporarily vacate our bodies, embarking on a sort of metaphysical sojourn—an out-of-body projection. Delving into this topic, the works of Robert A. Monroe, particularly his seminal book "Journeys out of the Body," shed light on the intricacies of such experiences.

Robert Allan Monroe, a former radio broadcasting executive, gained renown for his extensive research into altered states of consciousness, ultimately establishing "The Monroe Institute." His pioneering 1971 book, "Journeys out of the Body," played a pivotal role in popularizing the concept of out-of-body experiences.

Monroe's personal accounts, documented in books like "Ultimate Journey" and "Far Journey," provide valuable insights into his quest to comprehend the trajectory of his disembodied self. Although he automatedly induced out-of-body experiences, he did so without succumbing to death.

My own encounter with this phenomenon led me to attend one of Monroe's courses at the Monroe Institute in Virginia. These sessions aimed to teach participants how to consciously initiate and recollect their out-of-body experiences. Under hypnosis during the transitional state between wakefulness and sleep, I vividly experienced leaving my body and retained the memories of each occurrence.

During these courses, the instructors guided us in assisting entities in need of guidance, particularly those trapped in the earthly realm. I distinctly recall a poignant moment when I sought to visit a deceased client, a young girl, and through their guidance, I was able to communicate with her.

The cinematic portrayal of such experiences is captured in the movie "Somewhere in Time," featuring Christopher Reeve. In the film, Reeve's character hypnotizes himself to travel back in time, mirroring the power of focused consciousness. Returning to the present, paralleling my own experiences, evoked a sensation akin to the character's abrupt return.

Upon reintegration into my body, the shared mission, as understood, was to aid those who were spiritually adrift, facilitating their journey to their destined realms, be it heaven or elsewhere.

While Monroe's approach involved meticulous, one-on-one assistance, my own method evolved to a more efficient means of aiding earthbound entities. This adjustment allowed for a swifter and broader impact, transcending the limitations of individualized support during sleep.

This exploration into out-of-body experiences, marked by the ability to connect with the departed, proved to be an exhilarating and profoundly enlightening venture. The depth of understanding gained and the impact on those assisted underscored the transformative potential of exploring the mysteries that lie beyond the confines of the physical self.

How to Release Karma

Karma, deeply ingrained in various spiritual beliefs, revolves around the concept that our actions generate consequences governed by the principle of cause and effect. It holds that the culmination of one's deeds in both current and past lifetimes plays a pivotal role in shaping their destiny in future existences.

The law of cause and effect, an immutable force, operates on the understanding that individuals should not face punishment or obstruction due to their past actions. Instead, it embodies a law of love, seeking to liberate individuals from the constraints of their history—a history grounded in the belief of linear time, a concept confined to the past.

Empowering this understanding is the recognition that thoughts serve as the basis for decision-making. It is essential for each of us to grasp that we possess the capacity to choose our thoughts, thereby influencing the nature of our life experiences.

The potential for a beautiful and fulfilling life is universal, with peace and meaning constituting inherent birthrights. While spiritual growth may entail overcoming challenges, it is not limited to navigating painful obstacles.

Enlightenment, a state already present within, need not be contingent on a tumultuous existence. The act of reading and contemplating spiritual ideas signifies an existing connection with enlightenment. Lifestyle choices, whether conscious or subconscious, contribute to the experiences we encounter.

Instances of lack, limitation, or pain often indicate the influence of fearful thoughts within us. These thoughts may operate below our conscious awareness, necessitating a deliberate effort to gain control. Through practice, we can develop an acute awareness of our thoughts, discerning the nature of each moment's mental landscape. The experience of pain becomes a signal, indicating the presence of a fearful thought.

Spiritual progression involves a diminishing tolerance for pain, ultimately reaching a state of zero pain as fearful thoughts are relinquished. Recognition and release become second nature. Utilizing the support of angels or guides can provide the strength needed to embrace positive and loving thoughts consistently.

In the context of reincarnation and karma, there are instances where individuals may grapple with challenges without a clear understanding of their origin. To address this, the "Ho'oponopono" healing method is recommended. By placing hands over the heart and sincerely repeating the practice three times, individuals can release karmic burdens and promote healing, even in situations where the root cause may be elusive.

Moreover, attunement to Reiki is highlighted as an effective means of addressing karma. By dedicating oneself to the healing of others through the use of Universal energy, individuals can find forgiveness and liberation from karmic entanglements.

Healing one's way of thinking is acknowledged as a crucial aspect of this process, although it may pose challenges. Regular practice and a commitment to positive thinking contribute to a transformative shift. It is important to recognize that the law of attraction plays a role in our experiences, and some aspects of hardship may be linked to karmic influences.

Consideration of the homeless population serves as an illustration. Beyond the immediate lack of shelter or employment, their circumstances may be intertwined with karmic elements, presenting an opportunity for empathy and understanding within the broader spiritual framework.

Getting Over a Broken Heart

Navigating the challenging terrain of heartbreak can be an arduous journey. I share with you a method I employed to assist my sister through the profound anguish of a painful breakup with her deeply cherished boyfriend. Witnessing her overwhelming sorrow, I was compelled to alleviate her suffering and facilitate her healing process.

In the aftermath of the breakup, she found herself immersed in constant tears, struggling to carry on with daily life. The relentless replay of cherished memories compounded her distress, making it difficult for her to focus on essential aspects of life such as securing employment and maintaining well-being.

Understanding the profound difficulty of healing from such heartbreaks, characterized by a desire for the pain to cease—an emotional withdrawal akin to breaking an addiction—I endeavored to find a solution for my sister. The aim was to sever the attaching emotional loops and provide her with relief.

Drawing inspiration from the teachings of Sylvia Brown and insights from various literature on emotional healing, I embarked on a process involving the symbolic cutting of attaching emotional loops. Initially utilizing scissors and later transitioning to a crystal knife for enhanced efficacy, the process became an instrumental facet of the healing journey.

Recognizing the emotional intricacies attached to intimacy, particularly for women who tend to deepen their emotional connection post-intimacy, I guided my sister through a visualization exercise. It involved taking deep breaths and imagining the disconnection of her heart from the emotional ties associated with lovemaking.

Acknowledging the nature of female emotional attachment after intimacy—where women derive a sense of specialness and beauty—I explained the significance of preserving emotional well-being by detaching the heart chakra from the intimate aspects of the relationship.

Encouraging my sister to visualize the disconnection and reconnection at a time when she encountered a more suitable partner, I aimed to provide a sense of closure while maintaining an open heart for future love.

The exercise continued with a practical step—deleting pictures or contact information of the ex-partner. This act served as a symbolic closure and an anchor for emotional liberation. It was a crucial step, particularly if the relationship had definitively concluded.

The effectiveness of this method was evident in my sister's transformative experience. While memories of her past relationship persisted, the emotional pain associated with them dissipated significantly. The process was further reinforced by the act of deleting contact information, enhancing the overall efficacy of the healing approach.

Since then, this method has been employed with success for both women and men facing the aftermath of heartbreak. The results underscore the power of a thoughtful and intentional approach to emotional healing, providing solace and renewed hope for those traversing the challenging terrain of heartbreak.

5 UNIVERSAL POWER

Dreams, as enigmatic as they may seem, harbor a unique significance that is inherently tied to your individual experiences and emotions. While certain symbols may carry universal meanings, the true essence lies in decoding what each dream specifically means to you. The pivotal step in this process is initiating an evaluation of your dreams, a practice that commences as you wake, compelling you to meticulously document the dreams that resonate with significance.

Guidelines for Evaluating Your Dreams

While collective interpretations of universal symbols may offer a foundation for internal analysis and growth, my emphasis lies in exploring the nuanced directions dreamers take with these symbols and the personal connections they forge as a result. Even seemingly mundane dreams, such as envisioning a breakfast of oatmeal, can unfold profound insights when subjected to thoughtful scrutiny.

In the realm of dream evaluation, consider the intricacies that surround your encounter with oatmeal: the setting, emotions, and associations that spring forth. Questions like "Am I alone at breakfast?" or "Does this evoke memories of my mother's cooking?" can unravel layers of meaning. In this quest for understanding, delve into the specifics—flavors, textures, and contextual details—that transform an ordinary dream into a valuable source of introspection.

Unraveling the Tapestry of Dreams

Each dream, irrespective of its apparent simplicity, holds unique significance for you. Transcribe your dreams faithfully and embark on a journey of self-discovery by exploring their diverse meanings. Allow the interpretations to unfold organically, observing how they resonate with your inner self.

Certain dreams may manifest as repetitive or reparative, requiring heightened attention. These recurring dreams may harbor essential messages, and it is imperative to discern the underlying narratives they convey. Promptly document your dreams upon awakening, for the ethereal nature of these experiences renders them susceptible to fading into oblivion as the day unfolds.

Practical Tips for Dream Journaling

Establish the ritual of keeping a dream journal within arm's reach, ensuring immediate documentation upon waking. This repository becomes a valuable tool for discerning patterns, unraveling subconscious themes, and decoding the messages encapsulated in your dreams.

Personal Anecdote: The Co-worker's Dream

Reflecting on a personal encounter with dream interpretation, a dream involving a critical co-worker clad in a pink blouse with black spots unfolded. Subsequently, a large insect bearing the same color pattern emerged in the dream, met with an unthinking step. The revelation that this insect mirrored the co-worker was an uncanny realization.

Insight into Familiar Dream Patterns

Certain dream motifs, such as teeth falling out accompanied by blood, recurrently surface when someone close to me is expecting. Despite its cryptic nature, this recurring dream serves as an intuitive precursor to impending familial news.

Empowering Your Dream Interpretation Journey

While various interpretative resources exist, akin to tarot cards, they serve as aids rather than conclusive guides. Your dreams, a unique tapestry woven from personal experiences, require the application of interpretative tools that resonate with your inner self. Engage with your spiritual beings, be it angels or guides, to amplify your understanding of dream meanings—each response or insight bestowed upon you carries profound significance in the realm of self-discovery.

Have You Seen the Future?

Certain individuals possess the unique gift of foretelling events through dreams or visions, experiencing a sense of familiarity in novel surroundings—commonly referred to as deja-vu. Have you encountered such occurrences? The feeling that the present moment has been lived before is a classic manifestation of deja-vu.

Deja-vu, while often interpreted in paranormal contexts, faces skepticism in mainstream scientific circles regarding precognition or prophecy (Wikipedia). Let's delve into this intriguing phenomenon more explicitly, as it is likely that you, too, have grappled with its enigma. Moments when a dream intrudes upon your current activities, leaving you questioning, "Have I been here before?" or sensing an eerie familiarity, evoke a peculiar sensation.

For many, the ability to dream of future events is not uncommon. The experience can be perplexing, leaving you momentarily perplexed. If you find yourself in such a scenario, where your dreams seem to offer glimpses into the future, consider it a potential revelation of your purpose as a lightworker.

However, deja-vu isn't always a serene revelation. A personal encounter involved driving on a clear day, only to witness, through the mind's eye, a distressing vision of a young lady bound with duct tape inside a red truck with a silver trailer. The unsettling feeling of dreaming while driving raised questions about intervention.

In such moments, seeking guidance from one's highest self, guides, or angels becomes crucial. A discerning inquiry about intervention may arise, accompanied by a profound understanding that clear instructions will be imparted if intervention is warranted. Trusting your instincts, acting without overthinking, and receiving guidance from spiritual entities are integral aspects of navigating these unique experiences.

A poignant example emerges from a healing session where three troublesome entity attachments were encountered during an attempt to help someone overcome drug addiction. The unexpected sensation of entities passing through, akin to a scene from the movie "Ghost," left an indelible mark. The subsequent realization that this challenging experience was a premeditated lesson, a request initiated by the individual undergoing the healing, emphasized the importance of trust in divine guidance.

It is essential to recognize that spiritual beings and higher powers do not subject individuals to undue danger. Lessons and experiences may unfold unexpectedly, challenging our fears and egos. Maintaining open communication with spiritual entities and cultivating a connection with the divine ensures clarity and understanding amidst such spiritual journeys.

How do I find lost items?

Experiencing the loss of something deeply valued can be emotionally devastating. In my own life, I encountered a significant loss when I misplaced the $2,000+ phone my husband had gifted me. It happened during a large convention, where I inadvertently left my phone on a side table while engaged in conversation with a friend.

Upon realizing the absence of my phone, I immediately invoked the Divine white light and sought assistance from my angels and guides to aid in its recovery. I approached the convention organizers, and they agreed to check the lost and found section. Approximately an hour later, an announcement over the intercom summoned me to the lost and found area, where my phone was returned by a conscientious individual who had found it. Overwhelmed with gratitude, I extended blessings and the Divine white light to the honest person who had turned in my phone, appreciating the virtue of honesty.

Reflecting on this incident, I recall a similar event involving my Reiki friends. Their husband, laden with anxiety, had lost his wallet containing a substantial amount of money, credit cards, and his driver's license. Aware of my spiritual practices, his wife sought my assistance. Utilizing my pendulum, I listed the stores he had visited and, employing the Divine white light for protection, sought guidance to locate the lost wallet. The pendulum indicated that none of the stores held the missing wallet, dispelling concerns of permanent loss. A strong intuition led us to check his truck, where the wallet was discovered precariously wedged between the passenger truck door and an open compartment. This successful recovery left him elated, offering gratitude and dinner in appreciation.

In another instance, my brother faced the heartbreak of his truck being stolen, along with cherished tools stored in a silver toolbox. Following a session of Reiki and a petition to Mother Azna, a goddess figure, his prayers were for the recovery of the truck and its contents without any damage.

Miraculously, a call from the police station came one and a half weeks later, announcing the recovery of the truck with all tools intact and no harm done. This unexpected turn of events brought immense joy and relief, underscoring the power of spiritual tools and petitions.

These experiences serve as reminders of the myriad spiritual tools available to us, offering assistance and guidance in times of need. The simple act of asking and utilizing these tools can pave the way for unexpected miracles and resolutions to challenging situations.

Activation of Items for Positive Energy

In the realm of holistic practices, I have employed my Curandero skills for the purpose of activating items with positive energy. This includes diverse objects such as Angel figures, gemstones, vitamins, and medications. The activation process involves an initial assessment using my pendulum to evaluate the existing energy within these items. For instance, in the case of vitamin D3, I enhance its energy to compensate for the limited exposure to sunlight, a primary source of this essential nutrient.

The pendulum's clockwise circle size serves as a metric, revealing the energy level of the item. To activate vitamin D3, I utilize sacred symbols by inscribing them in the air and imbuing them into the bottle three times. The extension of the pendulum circle post-activation provides a tangible indication of the heightened energy, resulting in an instantly gratifying process.

Similarly, I extended this practice to Angel figures, including crystal, red, and golden angels. Placing them above the wall by my bed, I prayed and invoked their protection and positive energy. The pendulum, when applied for energy assessment, showcased widened clockwise circles post-activation with Reiki sacred symbols.

Positive energy activation is not limited to inanimate objects; I extend it to precious gemstones. Using Reiki symbols and prayer, I activate and infuse positive energy into them. The pendulum serves as a reliable indicator of the positive energy infusion.

However, a cautionary note emerged from my experiences. Placing positively energized gemstones in the bedroom can disrupt sleep due to an excess of energy. Consequently, I relocated these items to restore peaceful sleep.

Expanding the spectrum of positive energy activation, I incorporate prayer and sacred Reiki symbols for various purposes. This includes plants, my car, protection for my house, my children, grandchildren, friends, relatives, food, and even my body for healing and repair. The inclusion of the white light of the divine spirit source enhances the effectiveness of these practices.

To channel healing energy to individuals, I utilize small figures representing a man and a woman. Cupping these figures in my hands, I visualize the person in need, enveloping them in the divine white light and directing healing energy to specific areas of pain or illness. Prayer to their angels or spirit guides, along with connecting through my own angels, serves as a supplementary measure to assess the success of long-distance healing.

These practices, rooted in prayer and healing methodologies, offer versatile applications, encouraging the creative use of one's imagination. Consistency and patience in these endeavors yield positive outcomes, making these processes valuable components of holistic well-being.

How do animals fit into healing?

The role of animals in the context of healing has garnered increasing attention and significance. Notably, pets such as dogs and cats have been observed to mirror the health conditions of their owners, displaying a profound connection that goes beyond mere companionship. The depth of their bond is evident in instances where pets, driven by their love for their owners, seem to absorb or share in the emotional and physical ailments experienced by their human counterparts. Some pets even exhibit a striking resemblance to their owners, an intriguing phenomenon.

An illustrative example is the case of my daughter adopting a dog from an animal rescue mission. This canine companion, having lost its previous owner to cancer, subsequently succumbed to the same illness after a few months of living with my daughter. While peculiar, such occurrences underscore the profound emotional and empathetic ties that exist between humans and their animal companions.

Animals contribute to our well-being in ways that often go unnoticed. Beyond the conventional roles of companionship, they exhibit a natural instinct to provide healing. In instances where an individual has a cut or an open wound, a dog, in particular, may instinctively lick the affected area. This behavior is rooted in the belief that the saliva of animals possesses healing properties, and indeed, animals tend to groom and lick their own wounds as part of their self-healing process.

Recognizing the therapeutic potential of animals, some hospitals have embraced the practice of allowing dogs to interact with patients, especially the elderly and children. The presence of these animals has been found to bring comfort and support to patients undergoing medical treatment.

A fascinating dimension of the relationship with animals is the ability to communicate with them on a more profound level. Anecdotes such as the experience with a cat during a Reiki healing session highlight the potential for deeper connections. The cat, seemingly attuned to the energy work being conducted, mirrored the practitioner's hand movements throughout the session. Subsequent revelations about the mistreatment of the cat underscore the notion that animals may possess a form of communication that extends beyond conventional understanding.

This leads to the exploration of animal communication as a skill or gift. Instances of individuals, such as Anna Brentenbrach, becoming renowned animal communicators further underscore the possibility of tapping into this innate ability. The lost connection with nature, where humans and animals once communicated seamlessly, prompts reflection on the potential to rekindle this intrinsic connection through learning and practice.

The discovery of individuals offering classes to teach animal communication signifies a growing interest in reviving this inherent connection. Exploring such abilities could offer valuable insights into the profound relationship between humans and animals, potentially opening new dimensions of understanding and connection. The fascinating topic of animal communication, as explored by experts like Anna Brentenbrach, invites contemplation on the depth of our interconnectedness with the animal kingdom.

The Divine White Light, Why Use It?

In my interactions with various individuals, I often encounter discussions about the concept of the "Divine White Light." While many may not have an extensive understanding of angels, there is a widespread recognition of the white light and its perceived capabilities. Referred to as the "Divine White Light," it is frequently employed for its perceived power in healing, safeguarding, and shielding individuals from entities and negativity. Despite lacking comprehensive knowledge about its workings, many individuals are drawn to its potential benefits.

The potency of the Divine White Light is evident in numerous anecdotes highlighting its protective qualities. One poignant example involves a family whose home was invaded by U.S. Immigration and Customs Enforcement (ICE). In the face of this traumatic event, the family, guided by the principles of the Divine White Light, managed to avoid further apprehension, minimizing the impact of this distressing encounter. Such instances underscore the remarkable protective attributes attributed to the Divine White Light.

Amidst the complexities of immigration enforcement actions, individuals facing potential legal challenges have sought assistance. I encountered a client with a past DUI charge, discovered years later by ICE, prompting fear and uncertainty. Rather than pursuing legal avenues, I guided her in utilizing the Divine White Light for protection. Subsequently, she relocated, avoiding any further encounters with immigration authorities. This narrative emphasizes the practical application of the Divine White Light as a protective measure in challenging situations.

The process of invoking the Divine White Light is remarkably straightforward:

1. Close your eyes.
2. Envision surrounding yourself with the Divine White Light.
3. Extend this protective visualization to encompass areas or individuals you wish to shield, such as family members, pets, or your vehicle.

The simplicity of this ritual makes it accessible to anyone seeking added protection. Whether safeguarding against potential dangers like burglars or instilling a sense of security while driving, the Divine White Light serves as a versatile shield. It extends beyond personal protection to encompass broader intentions, such as sending healing energy to individuals undergoing surgery or contributing to the Earth's well-being.

In situations involving negative energy or encounters with unsettling individuals, the Divine White Light can be employed to establish a protective barrier. Its transformative potential even extends to making individuals "invisible" to those harboring harmful intentions.

For enhanced protection, individuals are encouraged to incorporate additional support from angels and guides. By consistently integrating the Divine White Light into daily routines, individuals can foster a sense of security and well-being. Whether facing workplace challenges or personal conflicts, the Divine White Light serves as a valuable tool for establishing boundaries and seeking assistance from higher spiritual realms.

In conclusion, the regular utilization of the Divine White Light for protection stands as a testament to its efficacy and practicality in navigating life's challenges.

6 MORTALITY

When Am I Going to Die?

Have you ever pondered the inevitable question: How will my life conclude? It is a common desire for many to envision a painless departure, perhaps peacefully in one's sleep, maintaining the illusion of a seamless transition from dreaming to eternal rest. However, from a spiritual standpoint, there exists a belief that the choices surrounding our departure are made before our earthly existence begins.

The understanding revolves around the notion that we, as spiritual entities, are afforded three to four opportunities to select the circumstances of our return home. These circumstances can manifest through accidents, attempts on our lives, the onset of diseases, or even the drastic decision to end one's own life. The key lies in the concept of choice during these pivotal moments.

Before our incarnation, a comprehensive life plan is believed to be crafted, delineating the contours of our life's purpose. This plan encompasses various aspects, such as our chosen profession, be it as a lawyer, doctor, healer, or teacher, with the overarching aim of impacting others positively. Some individuals are designated as crucial elements in the lives of others, entrusted with the responsibility to save or inspire someone whose destiny is intertwined with theirs.

The intricate web of connections extends to our current relationships—with parents, significant others, children, and even the animals in our lives. Each of these connections is believed to be deliberately chosen before our descent to Earth, contributing to the richness and complexity of our human experience.

In the formulation of this life plan, a celestial committee, guided by guardian angels, spirit guides, and sometimes ancestral figures, plays a pivotal role. These beings, connected to us across various lifetimes, serve as custodians of our life's purpose and the lessons we are meant to learn.

However, the extent to which our lives are meticulously planned varies. Some contend that nearly every step is preordained, while others argue that only major milestones are predetermined. Regardless, the involvement of guardian angels, spirit guides, and the celestial committee remains constant, offering guidance and intervention when necessary.

In instances where our lives may be threatened prematurely, these spiritual entities may intercede, especially if our lessons remain unlearned or our life purpose unfulfilled. They may guide us in making decisions that align with our greater purpose, ensuring that we persist until the next crucial juncture—referred to as an "intersection time."

A compelling personal account illustrates this phenomenon. Faced with a perilous encounter during a late-night assignment, the intervention of guardian angels became audible and directive. Sometimes our guardian angels and spirit guides will intervene if we are about to be killed and without our permission especially if we have not learned our lessons or it is not our time to die. If our "intersection time" comes up they will help us make a decision especially if we have not completed our purpose or learned the lessons we are to learn.

We will decide to stick around until our next "intersection" comes around. I remember when I was working with a client that no one else wanted to work with. I was working the graveyard shift and I needed to get this client his meds.

It was getting pretty late, and I knocked on his door and he grabbed me and said "you will have to do!" He threw me on the floor and started to take my clothes off, I screamed but I knew no one would be able to hear me.

I very clearly heard my angle guides say really loud "tell him you don't like white men". I thought "Oh, I can't say that he will kill me!" as I was struggling with him, I heard them say again, only louder. "TELL HIM YOU DON'T LIKE WHITE MEN!!! I yelled this to the client, and he jumped off me, gave me my clothes and I ran out. I did not know at that time, they were my guardian angels, yelling at me.

I told my supervisor the next day what had happened, and they took him off my assignment. It turned out he was a very dangerous client who had a very bad criminal record and that was why others did not want to work with him.

But I was raising three children by myself, and they were paying good money for that shift and I could see my children before they left to school in the mornings and for two hours at night before they went to bed.

I did feel however, that was one of the times that I could have made a choice to ignore them, but on their second warning, I made the choice to listen to them. That is what saved my life. I feel that was one of the "intersection" times.

In conclusion, the exploration of pre-birth planning, spiritual entities, and the concept of "intersection" times invites contemplation on the orchestrated nature of our earthly journey. It encourages individuals to reflect on the profound influence of spiritual guidance during pivotal moments, acknowledging the intricate tapestry of connections that shape our human experience.

Our Deceased Loved Ones

In the aftermath of losing cherished individuals, it is worth considering the profound possibility that they continue to linger in our lives even after crossing over. By invoking prayers for their peaceful transition, we unlock the potential for heightened assistance from our departed loved ones. Post-transition, they gain increased capacity to support us in various aspects, provided we seek their guidance from the celestial realms.

During the initial 90 days following their passing, souls may choose to remain in close proximity before deciding on their subsequent course of action. This pivotal juncture offers them the autonomy to determine whether to linger and fulfill a unique mission or proceed to their next assignment. Some souls willingly volunteer as guides for their living loved ones, driven by a deep-seated care and commitment to their well-being.

For those who bear the namesake of departed loved ones, an intriguing connection unfolds. Named after a departed relative, individuals may find themselves accompanied by a spirit guide who shares similarities in soul path and purpose. This ethereal guide, often having undergone a spiritual counselor training program in the celestial realm, abides by the principles of providing support without infringing upon free will.

In the heavenly school of spiritual development, these guides learn the art of astral travel, maintaining proximity for communication through dreams, inner voices, gut feelings, and intellectual insights. Additionally, they harness the power of the third eye to convey visions, daydreams, or mental images, fostering a subtle yet impactful connection with the living.

Occasionally, departed souls may remain unaware of their transition. A poignant example involves an elderly uncle who, in his final years, succumbed to the sedative effects of pain medication. Following his peaceful passing at the age of 93, attempts to contact him revealed a slumbering state in the afterlife. Through intentional communication, his spiritual awakening unfolded as he was gently guided to acknowledge his transition and embrace the freedom from pain.

The process involved encouraging him to explore his newfound spiritual existence, leveraging imagination to dress as desired. This intervention facilitated his transition into the spirit world, a realm where he could manifest the attire of his choice. Ensuring his spiritual awakening through clear communication and the use of a pendulum, the connection was solidified, allowing him to reunite with his family and fulfill his higher purpose.

The subsequent involvement of his spirit guides, who have accompanied him across multiple lifetimes, ensured his seamless integration into the spiritual realm. This collaborative effort culminated in his presence at the funeral service and reception, affirming the successful completion of his earthly assignment.

While the physical absence may be keenly felt, the enduring spiritual connection offers solace and the assurance of his continued happiness and well-being. The reciprocal gratitude expressed by the departed soul underscores the profound impact of maintaining this spiritual bridge between the living and the departed.

Reunited with Stillborn Children

Encountering a client grappling with the emotional aftermath of pregnancy loss, my primary objective was to provide support and healing. This client, who initially sought assistance in conceiving, faced the heart-wrenching experience of losing twins before full term. Subsequently, her emotional well-being suffered, prompting her return to seek solace and guidance.

Recognizing her profound desire for motherhood and the emotional toll of the loss, I proposed utilizing hypnotherapy to facilitate a connection with her departed twins in a healing context. Assuring her that this process did not involve any harm or danger, I assessed her susceptibility to hypnosis and found her to be a receptive candidate for the therapeutic intervention.

With her consent, I initiated a specialized hypnosis technique known as "the climbing up some steps to heaven induction." This method guided her through a symbolic journey to heaven, where cleansing mist and forgiveness awaited her. The cleansing process was designed to alleviate any lingering guilt or self-blame associated with the loss of her twins.

Witnessing tears of relief during this process, the client conveyed a profound sense of forgiveness and release from burdensome emotions. Transitioning to a serene meadow adorned with vibrant exotic flowers, she was encouraged to pick flowers for her departed twins, fostering a sense of connection and love.

As she sat on a bench, two silhouettes approached her in the heavenly realm. Revealing themselves as a boy and a girl, they invited her to play, offering moments of joy and interaction. After granting her privacy for this poignant reunion, she tearfully recounted the emotional exchange. The twins assured her that they would be reunited in the future, leaving her with a sense of peace and closure.

Remarkably, this therapeutic hypnotherapy session had a transformative impact on her emotional state. The client reported a significant reduction in depression and expressed gratitude for the positive change in her outlook. This holistic approach not only addressed her emotional wounds but also paved the way for renewed hope.

Four months following this healing session, she successfully conceived and welcomed a baby boy into her life. The journey towards motherhood was celebrated in a baptism ceremony, where she extended an invitation to express her gratitude. This multifaceted approach, combining hypnotherapy, emotional healing, and spiritual connection, exemplifies the potential for holistic methods to empower individuals on their paths to recovery and fulfillment.

Do all babies go to heaven?

Offering condolences for the profound loss of a child, it's a deeply challenging experience that elicits immense grief. The desire to comprehend the fate of infants, whether stillborn, lost in the womb, or through abortion, sparks various interpretations rooted in religious beliefs and personal convictions. In such moments, the emphasis should lie not in establishing a singular truth but in finding solace through individual healing mechanisms.

Amid diverse explanations prevalent in religious texts and online discourse, the focus should shift towards whatever brings solace and aids the healing process. Personal experiences often shape our perspectives on these matters. One example involves my mother's experience with twin pregnancies, cut short before full term. Subsequently, she gave birth to a boy on 8/13/1960 and a girl on the same date in a subsequent pregnancy—an occurrence that transcends statistical probability and hints at the mysterious workings of fate.

Observing such occurrences as divine interventions, it becomes evident that certain souls are destined to join specific families to fulfill their unique life purposes. This perspective aligns with the notion that souls choose their parents, and if not welcomed in one incarnation, they may seek a similar familial link to complete their karmic journey.

Another poignant illustration emerges from a therapeutic encounter with a client who lost twins and sought assistance in overcoming the ensuing depression. Employing clinical hypnotherapy, I guided her through a transformative session where her twins communicated that they would return, albeit one at a time. Subsequently, she bore a son and then a daughter, affirming the fulfillment of the communicated message.

Similarly, another client's journey involved multiple losses when her circumstances were not conducive to welcoming a child. However, as her situation evolved, and her mindset shifted, she embraced the prospect of parenthood, leading to the successful birth of twins.

These narratives, albeit deeply personal, underscore the idea that souls may re-enter the world through the same or different parents, guided by a cosmic plan or chart. The intricacies of these spiritual phenomena, as gleaned from therapeutic experiences, suggest a profound connection between the souls and the chosen parents.

In conclusion, the question of whether all babies go to heaven transcends conventional understanding. Instead, it delves into the complex interplay of destiny, soul choices, and familial bonds. The narratives shared here underscore the profound nature of these experiences, highlighting the potential for healing, rebirth, and the intricate dance between the spiritual realm and human existence.

Reiki helps grieving.

In light of recent news about the passing of my beloved uncle, I find solace in sharing insights on the grieving process and the role Reiki has played in my personal healing journey.

Anticipating his impending departure, I visited my uncle at his residence, sensing the frailty in his health. During our meeting, he expressed a desire to visit me soon, a promise that resonated deeply. In the realm of grieving and healing, Reiki emerged as a comforting companion, drawing upon my Curandera skills to establish a connection with my departed loved one.

Grief, an indescribable weight on the heart, prompted me to explore new avenues for solace. I decided to incorporate a Reiki ritual, a departure from my usual practices but a testament to the adaptability of this healing modality. Emphasizing to my students the personalization of Reiki, I embarked on a ritual aimed at honoring my uncle's journey beyond.

Creating a modest altar adorned with his picture, I applied Reiki symbols, culminating in the use of Hon-Sha-Ze-Sho-Nen—the long-distance healing symbol—acknowledging his transition to another dimension. As I knelt, enveloped in the divine white light, I invoked the presence of my Angels, Reiki guides, and spirit guides for companionship on this spiritual journey. The meditation served as a conduit to communicate my well-wishes for his celestial sojourn, reuniting with family, especially my mother and beloved Tia Paula.

Expressing gratitude for the cherished moments we shared, I envisioned him embracing our departed family members. Engaging in a heartfelt conversation, I felt his ethereal presence, answering his inquiries with the best of my knowledge. Concluding the ritual, I left a burning candle as a symbolic continuation of the connection established.

Attending my uncle's funeral surrounded by grieving family, I contemplated the delicate nature of expressing condolences. Grief can manifest in diverse ways, prompting some friends to withdraw, and certain family members to avoid conversation. It is not a reflection of indifference but a testament to the profound pain endured.

Recalling the isolation I felt after my sister's passing, where mentioning her name evoked tears, I sought to spare my cousins a similar sense of abandonment. The intricacies of grief underscore the importance of empathy and understanding, acknowledging the discomfort that words may bring and providing silent support when words fall short.

In sharing this personal journey, I hope to illuminate the multifaceted nature of grief and the nuanced ways Reiki, adapted to personal needs, can offer solace amidst profound loss.

In times of mourning, it is crucial to prioritize self-care and emotional well-being. To those navigating the loss of a loved one, the following guidelines are offered for consideration:

1. **Prioritize Physical Health**: Ensure that your physical health is maintained through regular self-care practices.

2. **Maintain Routine:** Adhere to your daily routines, including regular sleep patterns, even if rest may be elusive.

3. **Engage in Meditation and Prayer**: Dedicate moments to meditation or prayer, creating a sacred space to honor and remember your loved one.

4. **Cultivate Joy and Gratitude**: Reflect on the moments of joy and express gratitude for the time spent with your loved one.

5. **Embrace Emotional Expression**: Allow yourself to cry as a natural and cathartic means of emotional expression; the act of crying contributes to the healing process.

6. **Share Memories**: Openly discuss your loved one with those who understand the profound impact of losing someone dear.

7. **Allocate Personal Time**: Carve out moments for self-reflection and solitude, acknowledging the importance of personal time.

8. **Avoid Prolonged Isolation**: While solitude is essential, refrain from isolating yourself for extended periods; seek connections with others when you feel ready.

9. **Seek Comfort**: Do not hesitate to seek comfort in the form of a hug or supportive embrace.

In expressing these sentiments, I extend my gratitude for allowing me to share in your mourning process. The presence of someone to talk to and share tears with can provide a meaningful source of solace during challenging times.

What do angels think of suicide?

The profound impact of losing a friend or relative to suicide can be overwhelming, prompting complex thoughts and emotions. Reflecting on the beliefs surrounding suicide, it's essential to consider a compassionate perspective:

1. **Heavenly Support:**

- Negative claims about those who take their own lives are challenged. The higher power, angels, and heavenly assistants provide support akin to mental health counselors.
- The departed are enveloped in the comforting presence of angels, undergoing spiritual healing and guidance.

2. **Spiritual Transformation:**

- Individuals who commit suicide may embark on a journey of spiritual transformation. They are offered choices, such as becoming spirit guides or returning to Earth to achieve success.

3. **Posthumous Reflection:**

- Our prayers serve as a source of upliftment and healing for those who have transitioned. They reflect remorse for causing pain to loved ones and seek forgiveness from themselves.

4. **Coping with Guilt:**

- Coping with guilt on Earth can be challenging. Recognizing guilt as a form of self-disrespecting a loved one's free will is crucial.
- Forgiving oneself is a necessary step in the healing process, acknowledging the complex emotions that accompany loss.

5. **Support for the Bereaved:**

While well-intentioned, expressions like "time will heal all" may inadvertently dismiss current feelings of pain. Engaging in practical initiatives, such as creating a GoFundMe page or joining Suicide Prevention groups, can be impactful.
Visiting memorials and finding ways to honor the departed contribute to the healing journey.

6. **Continuous Connection:**

Communication with the departed is ongoing. Signs, such as the appearance of a butterfly or encountering a familiar scent, serve as indications that our loved ones are listening.
Embracing the belief that our departed loved ones regain free will enables them to choose their spiritual path, potentially returning as family members in subsequent lifetimes.

7. **Support Resources:**

For individuals grappling with suicidal thoughts, the National Suicide Prevention Lifeline at 1-800-273-8255 offers crucial support. In emergencies, dialing 9-1-1 is imperative.

Approaching the subject of suicide with empathy and understanding can contribute to a collective effort in fostering healing and support for those affected.

7 EMPOWERMENT

In another chapter, I talked to you about practicing your magic talents. Like everything in life. It takes practice. So, practice magic.

Practice Magic

Embarking on the journey of learning energy sending is akin to acquiring the skills of driving. In the initial stages, the process may seem intricate, much like navigating mirrors while learning to drive. However, with dedicated practice, it evolves into a seamless, almost instinctive ability.

Much like the transition from a novice driver to a seasoned professional, sending positive energy becomes second nature. The key lies in practicing regularly, trusting your instincts, and believing in the unwavering support of your guides and angels.

Consider the narrative of safeguarding a loved one, a practice exemplified through personal experience. Requesting the presence and protection of a guide or angel, such as the author's angel named "AyaKita," illustrates the accessibility of these celestial beings at our beck and call.

The connection with guides and angels extends beyond specific circumstances. It is an ongoing relationship that evolves as practitioners become attuned to their unique energies. Recognition becomes intuitive, as demonstrated by the author when sensing the familiar energy of AyaKita upon their daughter's return.

For those immersed in the realm of Reiki, the acquisition of guides and angels is a profound aspect. Each attunement gifts practitioners with an additional guide/angel, offering a total of three to four companions. These celestial allies are not exclusive to Reiki practitioners; everyone may have two to three guides at any given time.

Guided practices involve self-care, enveloping oneself in the divine white light, and extending this protective energy to loved ones and the Earth. The magic of the world, often overlooked, encompasses healing elements present even in nature. Trees, for instance, offer solace and healing. Hugging a tree during moments of anxiety or overwhelming emotions allows for an exchange of energy, transforming negativity into positivity.

Recognizing the invaluable contributions of trees, from purifying the air to providing resources, underscores the interconnectedness of nature and our well-being. Energy sending extends beyond personal circles to include the Earth, reinforcing the notion that we are surrounded by healing helpers—our angels and guides.

In essence, the practice of sending loving energy is a transformative journey, fostering a profound connection with the celestial realm and the natural world.

How Can I Heal Myself?

The capacity for healing oneself is a journey intertwined with personal beliefs and perceptions. Frequently, we find ourselves mired in negative self-talk, criticizing our appearance, physique, or self-worth. The pivotal question emerges: How often do we harbor positive thoughts about ourselves?

Self-reflection prompts consideration of whether one feels unworthy or not good enough, and, more crucially, for whom and according to what standards. The influence of self-perception extends beyond the realms of the mind, permeating the mental, emotional, and physical facets of our being.

Remarkably, the mind possesses the capability to shape our reality, both positively and negatively. Instances of psychosomatic illnesses arising from our thoughts are not uncommon. Our attitudes towards life, relationships, finances, and various stressors significantly impact our well-being.

The power of our thoughts to mold our physical state is exemplified in everyday scenarios. A positive start to the day can dissipate as the mind becomes entangled in concerns about impending responsibilities, transforming a once good mood into one laden with worry.

This shift in mindset can manifest physically, contributing to sore throats, colds, and overall health deterioration. The correlation between negative thoughts and physical ailments underscores the interconnectedness of mental and physical well-being.

Self-healing necessitates carving out dedicated time for introspection and meditation. In the pursuit of healing, the following steps can be instrumental:

1. **Create a Personal Sanctuary**:

- Designate a private space for self-reflection.
- Even a brief respite in a secluded bathroom can suffice.

2. **Engage in Guided Meditation**:

- Allocate 15 to 20 minutes for focused meditation.
- Begin with four intentional breaths, counting to six on the fourth breath while releasing tension.

3. **Visualization Technique**:

- Identify the area of discomfort or pain.
- Envision bathing it in the divine white light, maintaining focus despite the intrusion of distracting thoughts.

4. **Repetition and Discipline**:

- Acknowledge the challenge of overcoming mental interference.
- Cultivate self-discipline through consistent practice.

5. **Concluding the Session**:

Close the session with four intentional breaths, holding the breath to the count of six on the fourth repetition.

Repeat until the discomfort subsides.

The efficacy of this self-healing practice is demonstrated through personal anecdotes. In instances of serious illnesses, consistent focus on the divine white light facilitated healing within a span of three days. Similarly, a client facing surgery for colon polyps witnessed their disappearance after adopting this meditation technique.

These experiences underscore the potency of positive thinking and focused intention in the realm of self-healing. The amalgamation of prayer, Reiki, and a positive attitude has the potential to transform and alleviate ailments.

In essence, self-healing is an iterative process that requires dedication, discipline, and an unwavering commitment to fostering a positive mindset. The stories of personal triumph serve as testaments to the transformative power inherent in aligning one's thoughts with the pursuit of well-being.

Manifestation

The universe, an expanse of boundless abundance, is ready to bestow its goodness upon those who dare to ask and are prepared to receive. However, the act of receiving, seemingly straightforward, often proves challenging for many. A perplexing phenomenon emerges when individuals are offered money or a gesture of kindness, prompting them to respond with a hesitant, "No, it's okay." Why does this transpire, particularly among women? Is it an ingrained belief that they are undeserving of asking for or receiving good things?

While socioeconomic challenges, such as poverty and homelessness, may have karmic underpinnings, the ability to manifest abundance is a skill that can be cultivated. Despite its seemingly simple premise, the complexity arises from the constant stream of thoughts that occupy our minds. Through the iterative processes of remembering, contemplating, and discussing, thoughts metamorphose into potent beliefs, shaping our predominant vibrational patterns.

Enter the "Law of Attraction." This universal law posits that the thoughts we focus on emit vibrational frequencies, eliciting emotional responses that become dominant in our vibrational patterns. When a particular thought is revisited and ingrained, it becomes the prevailing vibrational pattern within us. This pattern, in turn, plays a pivotal role in attracting experiences that align with it.

Recognizing this, one must strive to elevate their own vibrations to align with their desired manifestations. The key lies in fostering positive attitudes, love for oneself and others, and cultivating an internal landscape filled with love, joy, and happiness. The pursuit of control over external circumstances and others proves futile, as the creative power lies solely in one's ability to shape their own life experiences.

In the quest for abundance, it is paramount to acknowledge and manage one's vibrations, keeping desired attractions close while relinquishing control over external forces. The universe demands a simple yet profound offering: a positive attitude and genuine love, both for oneself and others. As thoughts are powerful conduits, individuals are urged to articulate their desires and aspirations clearly.

Remember, the universe operates on the principle of reciprocity. What is put out into the cosmic expanse through thoughts is destined to return. By articulating one's desires with emotional intensity and a genuine yearning for happiness, the universe responds in kind. The key is to boldly ask for what is truly desired, ushering in a realm of abundance and fulfillment.

How to Check Your Chakras

Are you interested in exploring the intricacies of chakras and discovering how to assess and balance them effectively? Chakras, ancient repositories of spiritual wisdom dating back to 1500 BC, are integral to our well-being, influencing both the emotional and physical aspects of our energies. To delve into this profound realm, one must comprehend the seven major chakras that serve as vital energy centers.

The process of checking and healing chakras serves as a valuable starting point for understanding and addressing physical and emotional imbalances within the body. These spinning disks of energy, intricately connected to nerves, organs, and various body areas, require alignment and openness to maintain optimal functionality.

Embarking on the journey of chakra healing, the practitioner focuses on the seven main chakras, each representing distinct aspects of energy. For instance, the heart chakra, when closed or compromised, may indicate emotional wounds or relationship disruptions. The size and movement of the energy circle spin can provide insights into the nature and severity of the issue.

Utilizing a pendulum as a diagnostic tool, a small circular spin may signify minor emotional disturbances, while a lack of movement indicates a fully closed chakra. This closure could result from a range of relationships, extending beyond romantic involvements to familial connections.

A systematic examination of each chakra, coupled with mental visualizations, unveils the energy landscape within the practitioner or the individual under consideration. Subsequently, the practitioner employs talk therapy or Curandera ritual healing to address the identified issues and facilitate the reopening of closed chakras.

Self-awareness and personal healing are essential components of this practice. When practitioners sense imbalances within themselves, they undergo a similar diagnostic process. Utilizing a familiar and energetically charged space, such as a bed, they mentally visualize their body and pinpoint areas of density or stagnation. Employing a pendulum or intuitive sensing, they identify specific chakras requiring attention.

The subsequent steps involve the application of appropriate Sacred Reiki symbols to open closed chakras, initiating a spiritual healing process that contributes to sustained openness. Through meditation and introspection, practitioners unravel the root causes of energy blockages, seeking guidance from spirit guides if necessary.

The holistic perspective cultivated through this practice enables individuals to perceive themselves with newfound depth, integrating layers of energy and consciousness. By acknowledging the supreme wisdom within their divine spark, practitioners gain insights that guide daily life, fostering growth and development. Regular self-assessment ensures ongoing energetic equilibrium, empowering individuals on their journey of self-discovery and healing.

Child Healed from Nightmares

I received a phone call from a woman, whom I had encountered once before. She was related to one of my clients and sought an appointment to address her eight-year-old son's persistent nightmares. The child had been experiencing disrupted sleep, frequently waking up in distress, yearning to seek comfort by sleeping with his parents. The mother expressed concerns about the vivid dreams involving the violent demise of his parents by uniformed men.

Employing the Divine white light for protection and invoking my spirit companions, I initiated a conversation with the child, named Carlitos. Delving into his thoughts about God and angels, drawn from Bible school teachings, I aimed to understand the emotional and psychological roots of his distress.

Upon discussing the matter further with his parents, I explored potential triggers for Carlitos' nightmares. I inquired whether the family had engaged in discussions about safety measures, particularly in response to concerns about Immigration and Customs Enforcement (ICE). It became apparent that the family had implemented a safety plan, including a family meeting, to address potential encounters with immigration authorities.

While the parents shared insights, I engaged Carlitos in a calming activity, providing him with bubbles to play with. During this time, he enthusiastically participated, shouting out colors and expressing joy. However, when asked to recount one of his dreams, Carlitos became emotional, narrating a distressing scenario of losing his parents.

To alleviate his fear and anxiety, I introduced a visualization technique using the protective imagery of a bubble. Guiding Carlitos to associate the bubble with divine protection, we practiced deep breathing and visualization exercises. The goal was to empower him to create a mental sanctuary, shielded by God and angels, whenever he felt scared.

After multiple practice sessions, Carlitos exhibited increased comfort and confidence in utilizing the protective bubble visualization. His parents reported positive changes, with Carlitos voluntarily invoking the "bubble" technique before bedtime. The newfound coping mechanism not only brought relief to Carlitos but was also shared with his siblings.

In a subsequent update, the mother expressed gratitude, noting that the family had experienced a sense of relief as ICE had not pursued any actions against them. This case illustrates the potential impact of integrating visualization and coping techniques to address childhood nightmares, fostering a sense of security and empowerment in the face of challenging circumstances.

As a seasoned Curandera, Reiki Master, and Clinical Hypnotist therapist, I share this experience with the hope of inspiring others to explore alternative approaches to healing and supporting those in need.

Relief for fussy baby

I encountered a distressed client who sought assistance for their inconsolable baby suffering from colic, causing three sleepless nights. Observing a sunken and flat soft spot, known as "la moiera," at the center of the baby's head, I identified a potential factor contributing to the discomfort.

With the hope of addressing a possible alignment issue, I worked on the baby's soft spot, aiming to bring it to the appropriate level.

During the brief 15-minute treatment, the baby exhibited fussiness, yet, following the adjustment of the soft spot, the infant promptly fell asleep. Subsequent feedback from the parents revealed that the baby's fussiness had ceased, and she enjoyed a restful night, free from colic-related distress.

While some may find this practice unfamiliar, and its underlying mechanisms remain unknown, it has demonstrated efficacy in addressing infant discomfort associated with the soft spot. In instances where the soft spot has been sunken for an extended period, additional measures, such as applying a mixture of leathered-up hand soap and rosemary herb, are employed to support the spot until it naturally aligns with the rest of the baby's head.

As a Curandera, my role extends beyond the conventional, as illustrated by an invitation to a baptism celebration. At such gatherings, where joyous occasions are marked by music and dancing, I encountered a baby exhibiting distress, often attributed to the belief in the "evil eye." This phenomenon arises when someone with strong desire or intent gazes at the baby, unintentionally transmitting negative energy.

In this particular instance, I volunteered to use a traditional folk remedy involving an egg to counteract the effects of the evil eye. The intervention resulted in the baby falling asleep and awakening without any signs of discomfort.

While the concept of the evil eye may be perceived as a folk belief, personal experiences, such as those involving my late sister, have added a layer of mystery to this phenomenon. Her unintentional gaze led to the demise of guppies in a fish tank and, subsequently, baby birds in a friend's care. The unexplained nature of these occurrences raises questions about the potential influence of energy on living organisms, leaving room for further exploration and understanding in the future.

Do you need a mechanic?

It is a common practice to seek divine intervention when faced with car troubles, be it calling upon God or an angel for assistance in repairing a vehicle or finding an honest mechanic. In the realm of utilizing our spiritual connection for support in various aspects of life, I'd like to share a genuine story from a client who held profound affection for her aging 1981 pickup truck.

This client expressed a deep bond with her little truck, emphasizing how it had never left her stranded due to meticulous maintenance. However, a day came when a major repair was needed, and she took it to the dealership. To her dismay, they claimed the required part was unattainable due to the truck's age, suggesting she discard it and acquire a newer model as it was deemed worthless.

Overwhelmed with emotion, she sobbed, vowing never to part with her beloved truck and pledging to continue fixing it. As she recounted this emotional episode, she mentioned pulling over during her distress. Strangely, the windshield sprayer, which had never worked before, started functioning, spraying her windshield and compelling her to stop crying. The realization that her windshield sprayer was miraculously operational left her astounded and relieved.

In her state of emotional turmoil, she turned to Archangel Raphael, known as the king of healers, and Archangel Michael, seeking their assistance to find someone capable of working on her cherished truck. In that moment, she recollected an acquaintance who owned a similar vintage truck and had experience working on his own vehicle. Dialing him up from my office, she shared her predicament, and he agreed to assess the situation.

Two weeks later, during her next visit, she updated me on another issue, but this time, her 1981 pickup truck was running significantly better. She attributed the miraculous turnaround to the assistance of the Archangels, expressing immense gratitude for their intervention.

This poignant narrative resonates deeply with individuals who perceive their vehicles as more than mere modes of transportation but rather as integral parts of their lives. The belief in giving life, energy, and even a soul or spirit to cars is not uncommon, and the ability of these entities to respond to our requests out of love is considered a testament to the profound power of love itself.

The emotional connection we share with our vehicles, coupled with spiritual beliefs, continues to weave compelling stories of divine intervention and inexplicable occurrences that touch the hearts of those who hold such convictions.

Driving Protection on the Road

Our spiritual guides, Higher Self, and Angels serve as the paramount guardians on our journeys, especially when navigating the roads. Have you ever thought to seek protection before embarking on a car trip? Cultivating this practice can be immensely beneficial. Personally, before undertaking my monthly two-hour drive, my initial ritual involves invoking the protection of my divine sources, encompassing angels and guides, establishing a reassuring sense of security. Subsequently, I conscientiously fasten my seat belt, prioritizing safety.

In my routine, this pre-drive prayer not only instills a profound sense of well-being but also assures me of protection from potential issues, extending to the unlikely event of receiving a speeding ticket. Acknowledging my inclination to drive swiftly, often surpassing the speed limit by a modest margin, I am comforted by the understanding, shared by my brother, a police officer, that minor exceedances are typically tolerated.

Throughout the COVID-19 period, when road traffic was sparse, news reports indicated that, at their discretion, police officers refrained from stopping vehicles traveling at a safe 80 miles per hour. My prayerful requests extend beyond safe arrival but also involve divine intervention in interactions with law enforcement, ensuring their availability only when essential.

My heavenly protection has proven steadfast. On one occasion, as my alternator belt snapped, causing my car to overheat with smoke emanating from the hood, I found myself stranded. Alone on the roadside, my plea to divine sources was swiftly answered. Two kind-hearted Latino men, seemingly heaven-sent, offered assistance. Remarkably, they ingeniously fashioned a makeshift belt from one of my knee-highs, a temporary solution that allowed me to reach a garage safely.

As they escorted me to the service station, disappearing after ensuring my safe arrival, I couldn't help but feel that divine intervention had sent these compassionate souls to my aid. The creativity of using nylon knee-highs as a makeshift fan belt underscores the extraordinary ways in which divine protection manifests.

This narrative underscores the tangible impact of relying on spiritual entities — be they angels, guides, the Higher Self, or the divine — for protection. It serves as a testament to the unexpected forms divine assistance can take, leaving me with a profound appreciation for the protective forces that operate beyond our immediate comprehension.

8 TOOLS AND TECHNIQUES

Are gemstones or crystals magical?

The allure of gemstones and crystals extends beyond mere aesthetics; these remarkable minerals have the capacity to fortify and invigorate our energies. Are gemstones and crystals imbued with a certain magical quality? Many individuals carry these precious stones with them, finding that they enhance their strength and well-being. When activated with intent, these stones exhibit a heightened ability to heal or contribute to our overall health, fostering feelings of peace and a myriad of other experiences.

Allow me to share some of my favored gemstones. Among them is the amethyst, a member of the quartz family, exhibiting a captivating purple hue. Known for its purported ability to attract peace and dispel nightmares, it is often suggested to place this stone beneath one's pillow, particularly beneficial for preventing nightmares in children.

Another noteworthy gemstone is the aquamarine, which is associated with enhancing psychic powers and serves as the birthstone for March. Renowned for promoting peace and courage, it stands as a symbol of serenity. Additionally, the clear quartz crystal, recognized as one of the most powerful stones, is occasionally referred to as the "witches mirror." It is believed that gazing into this crystal can reveal glimpses of the future, and it is frequently employed in ceremonial wands by our Indian counterparts.

The utilization of copper, while not a stone, is worth mentioning for its health-promoting properties. Often worn as a bracelet, copper possesses both electrical and physical energy, despite its tendency to oxidize and temporarily discolor the skin when in contact with perspiration.

Coral, while technically not a stone, is employed for protection. Placed strategically on windowsills, doorways, and even in vehicles, coral is believed to shield against negative energies, entities, and individuals with malevolent intentions. The efficacy of these protective measures is attested to by various individuals.

A compelling anecdote involves the use of coral as a protective measure. In preparation for a visitor, the back door of my residence was left unlocked for her convenience. Activating the energy of the nearby coral stone, I intended to keep negative influences at bay. When the visitor encountered difficulty opening the door, I guided her through a calming exercise while holding the coral. Astonishingly, upon her renewed attempt, the door effortlessly opened, leaving her in awe of the stone's perceived influence.

Lastly, the "tiger's eye," a captivating yellow and brown stone, is associated with promoting wealth. Often embraced by gamblers seeking financial fortune, this stone's potential impact on financial matters has sparked interest.

Exploring my collection of gemstones is a delightful journey, as I rediscover the unique qualities and energies each possesses. Encouraging you to explore and understand the strengths of your favorite gemstones, their energetic powers can be both surprising and invigorating.

Have you heard of Ho'oponopono healing?

Ho'oponopono, derived from ancient Hawaiian shamanic traditions, is a profound practice aimed at healing various aspects of life. Translating to "to make things right or correct," Ho'oponopono addresses relationship issues, illnesses, and challenges stemming from karmic lessons in our current or past lives. The majority of life's challenges and negativity often result from stagnant energy or ancestral influences.

Through the opening of our hearts and embracing deep forgiveness, a transformative celebration can unfold. When consistently and reverently practiced on both oneself and others, Ho'oponopono has the potential to bring about rapid and dramatic changes in one's world.

Perhaps you've heard the remarkable story of Dr. Ihaleakala Hew Len, a Hawaiian therapist who cured an entire ward of criminally insane patients without direct interaction. Dr. Len's Ho'oponopono ritual involved placing one hand over his heart while reviewing patients' files and placing the other hand on the respective file. Uttering the words, "I am sorry, please forgive me, thank you, I love you," he healed them by initiating self-healing. The seemingly miraculous results highlight the potency of this practice.

The unique aspect of Ho'oponopono lies in its independence from specific knowledge about the individuals involved. Dr. Len had never met the patients but solely relied on the soulful intent expressed through the phrases. The empowering aspect of Ho'oponopono is its accessibility for personal use. It requires no external presence or audience; the words can be silently spoken within one's mind. The true power lies in the emotion and love accompanying the intention to seek forgiveness and love from the Universe.

Embarking on this life-changing journey does not demand an understanding of its intricacies. Ho'oponopono can become a personal healing method applicable to oneself, loved ones, or friends. The process involves:

- Placing your hand over your heart.
- Mindfully repeating the following words:
    - I am sorry.
    - Please forgive me.
    - Thank you.
    - I love you.
    - I love you.
    - I love you.

The energy flows through your heart with the pure intention to initiate healing. This technique holds the potential for application across diverse scenarios, whether directed towards a person of authority, a natural disaster, or a collective shift in consciousness.

Whenever a desire for change or something different arises, these heartfelt intentions and the repetition of the special words - "I am sorry," "Please forgive me," "Thank you," "I love you," "I love you," "I love you" - can wield powerful healing effects. These simple yet profound words can be easily memorized and serve as a potent tool for deep healing whenever needed. It reminds us of our shared responsibility for each other's healing, happiness, and joy in life.

Clearing of Energy Cords

Have you ever experienced feelings of fatigue, irritability, or even depression without a clear cause? If you work in a public-facing role, these emotions might be a result of absorbing negative energy from others. Professionals in helping roles, especially, are highly exposed to toxic emotions, making it crucial to regularly clear these energies through effective methods.

Consider implementing these proven techniques for clearing negative energy:

1. **Utilize Plants**:

    The simplicity of using plants makes it an effective method for clearing psychic debris. Grab a plant or lawn weed, remove it from the ground, and sweep it over yourself. Always express gratitude to nature for its clearing properties, returning the plant to the earth. Seeking assistance from Mother Azna and incorporating sacred Reiki symbols enhances the clearing process significantly.

    Plants, akin to converting carbon dioxide into fresh air, can absorb lower energies, making them valuable in ridding the body of energetic toxins. Incorporate live plants into your living space, and use symbols on the plant's soil to amplify their energy-transforming capabilities.

    For workspaces dealing with frequent interactions and potential negativity, strategically place plants to direct and absorb any released negative energy.

    Note: Ancient Chinese art suggests avoiding pointy or prickly leaves, as they are believed to hinder positive energy flow.

2. **Cord-Cutting**:

    Professionals offering acts of kindness may find that people form fear-based attachments, leading to energetic cords between individuals. These cords, resembling tubes, attach to various parts of the body, symbolizing a connection between individuals.

    Cord-cutting is a powerful method to release these attachments, particularly useful after a breakup or when dealing with clients who have just detached from significant others. Using symbolic representations of scissors or knives, either physically or through visualization, helps sever these cords and promote healing.

In instances where you feel drained or emotionally affected after helping someone, consider performing a cord-cutting ritual. By severing the toxic energy cords, you retain the positive, loving aspects of the relationship while eliminating the co-dependent and dysfunctional components.

Here's a simple process:

- Take a couple of deep breaths.
- Spend a few moments in silence.
- Breathe again, opening the door for angelic assistance.
- Relax and find peace within yourself.

Incorporating these techniques into your routine can contribute significantly to maintaining emotional and energetic balance, fostering overall wellness.

What is Dowsing?

Dowsing, a practice traditionally employed for locating water or hidden objects beneath the earth, has been utilized for many years. The classic tool associated with dowsing is the dowsing rod, which responds to the seemingly random movements of the person holding it. These movements are believed to be influenced by earth energy, guiding the dowser to specific points of interest.

In my practice, I employ a pendulum as an alternative to the traditional dowsing rod, finding it to be equally effective in energy assessment.

When clients reach out to me seeking prayers or insights into their well-being, I utilize a unique method involving drawing a stickman representation of their body. During this process, I surround myself with the divine holy white light and establish a connection with the client's angels and guides.

As I draw the stickman and inquire about the person's name and birthdate, I pay close attention to any irregularities in the drawing—jiggles, skips, dents, or darker printed areas. These nuances provide valuable information about the individual's energetic state.

This technique revealed its significance during an instance where my pen dented at the person's stomach area. Advising her to consult a doctor, it turned out she was unknowingly pregnant. The accuracy of the stickman method was validated when she reached out to confirm the findings.

In some cases, prior to meeting someone, I perform dowsing on that person to assess their physical well-being. Upon the scheduled appointment, I revisit the stickman drawing, checking off the insights obtained before the encounter. This practice often yields validations and contributes to a more informed session.

I learned this method from a Reiki Master healer during an interview for the "Luna Institute of Curanderos." This healer, who crafted a livelihood from selling healing herbs and ornaments sourced from nature, demonstrated the stickman method on me, leaving me fascinated and eager to integrate it into our institute's teachings.

Our paths intersect with various individuals possessing unique healing abilities, and some, like my esteemed teacher who recently passed away at the age of 84, leave an indelible mark on our lives. The stickman method, a means of exercising psychic abilities, serves as a valuable tool for ongoing practice and development.

While I cherish the memories of my old friends and teachers, I continue to explore and share my healing journey, always open to the mysteries and insights that emerge along the way.

How to Use a Pendulum

Pendulums serve as fascinating tools for seeking answers, offering individuals the ability to make selections based on energetic responses. In my teachings, I guide students on effectively using a pendulum to tap into their energy and trust their spirit guides for insightful responses.

While online resources or instructional books can provide assistance, creating a personalized pendulum adds a special touch. Crafting one with earthly materials allows for a unique and enjoyable experience, involving the selection of colors and special beads.

To establish a connection with my guides or angels, I initiate a prayer, aligning the pendulum with the desired responses for "yes" and "no." For instance, I set the pendulum to swing forward and backward for "yes" and left to right for "no," mimicking the natural nodding of the head.

Alternatively, one can opt for clockwise for "yes" and counterclockwise for "no." Once this calibration is achieved, users are ready to pose yes or no questions.

A stationary pendulum indicates a lack of information or uncertainty, prompting the acknowledgment that answers are currently unavailable. When seeking reassurance about an answer, I request the pendulum to swing wider, providing additional insights, especially concerning the timing of future events.

For time-related inquiries, such as appointments or upcoming occurrences, I utilize a clock face as a reference. Placing the pendulum on it assists in obtaining specific details. Similarly, a calendar aids in determining suitable dates for special events, streamlining planning efforts.

Occasionally, individuals approach me to seek answers through the pendulum. In such instances, I initiate a prayer, connecting my guides with the person's guides to facilitate accurate responses. The pendulum's movements, such as a tight circle, may convey the likelihood of an event, signifying a small chance of occurrence.

It is crucial to train one's guides on preferred methods of communication to ensure consistent and reliable answers. Additionally, users should be mindful of their own influence on the pendulum's responses. Detaching from the question and thinking about unrelated matters prevents unintentional influence and encourages accurate readings.

Beyond divination, some individuals employ the pendulum to assess the energy of substances like vitamins, medications, or food. Utilizing yes or no questions, this method serves as a valuable tool for intuitive decision-making.

While using the pendulum, it's important to exercise caution and remain open to the intuitive process. Detaching from the question and enjoying the experience fosters a more authentic and accurate use of this insightful tool.

What is Muscle Testing?

Muscle testing, akin to pendulum use, involves using one's fingers to test the body's responses for yes or no answers. Those familiar with the technique often engage in practice sessions to hone their skills. While effective, the success of muscle testing is believed to be contingent upon an individual's energy and mental state.

Requesting guidance from one's higher self, guides, and angels is essential in ensuring accurate outcomes, paralleling the approach used with pendulum work. Similar to pendulum use, personal influence on the answer must be minimized. Distracting oneself with unrelated thoughts, such as recalling breakfast or contemplating dinner plans, helps remove personal energy from the process.

The technique involves forming closed-ring circles with the thumb and middle finger of each hand, linking them together like a two-linked chain. The decision to designate one hand as "yes" and the other as "no" should remain consistent to avoid confusion. In this method, the pressure hand remains closed for "yes," while the resistance hand opens for a "no" response.

Alternatively, both circle fingers can be intended to remain locked for a "yes" answer and break for a "no" answer. Experimenting with the amount of resistance while making positive or negative statements helps identify the strength setting that allows the fingers to pull apart on a negative statement and stay linked on a positive statement.

Another less common method involves body swaying, a technique historically employed to discern truth from falsehood. In ancient times, a high priest's body swaying forward indicated truth, while swaying backward suggested falsehood or negativity. This method, while less prevalent today, can still be practiced by closing one's eyes and asking yes or no questions, observing the body's natural sway.

The extended arm method, employing downward pressure on the arm, is a popular alternative. These methods provide a glimpse into the variety of muscle testing techniques available.

While the aforementioned methods offer a comprehensive overview, there may be more variations worth exploring for those intrigued by the subject. Further information can be found through additional research on reputable sources, including the internet.

How to Smudge Your Home

Energy clearing, often referred to as house clearing, room smudging, or saging, is a widely acknowledged practice for eliminating negative energy within living spaces. This becomes especially relevant after intense and potentially volatile situations, such as heated arguments, leave lingering negative energy in a home. As a practitioner in the field, I, as a Curandera, often perform house-clearing sessions for clients.

To effectively clear negative energy from your home, it is advisable to utilize sage or lavender, which can be purchased or prepared at home. The preparation involves drying the leaves or sticks for approximately two weeks, or acquiring already dried products from a reputable source. Before commencing the process, it is crucial to invoke divine protection by surrounding yourself with the Divine white light.

Incorporating spiritual elements, such as prayer and symbols, enhances the effectiveness of the clearing process. A Reiki Master may use symbols like Sei-He-Ki and Cho-Ku-Reis to activate the sage or lavender, infusing them with the intent to cleanse the space and expel negative energies, entities, and any other unwelcome energies.

Here is a structured approach to smudging:

1. Begin by moving through every room in the house, allowing the smoke from the sage or lavender to permeate the space.
2. Focus on areas around windows, thoroughly smudging over and around them.
3. Attend to every corner of each room, ensuring that the entire space is smudged.
4. Extend the process to closets, leaving doors open if applicable.
5. Pay particular attention to the bathroom, a space where energies are often released.
6. If possible, open windows or doors to allow the smoke to exit the home.
7. Utilize bathroom fans or air vents to facilitate the removal of smoke if open windows are not feasible.

Homes, especially older ones, may retain energy from past occupants, especially if negative experiences or frequent arguments occurred. This residual energy can manifest as discarnates or "ghosts." While smudging, continue to pray, seeking ongoing assistance in clearing negative energies as they arise.

Additionally, when acquiring second-hand items, especially from garage sales or other people's homes, it is advisable to use a pendulum to check for attachments or negative energy. This precaution is essential to maintain a positive and harmonious living environment. Always remember that items received as gifts with genuine love are generally free from negative attachments.

Incorporating these professional guidelines can significantly contribute to creating and maintaining a positive and energetically balanced home environment.

Long-distance Healing

Have you ever wished for the well-being of a loved one, closing your eyes and sending healing thoughts? The power of love and positive energy transcends physical boundaries, manifesting as what is commonly known as Long-Distance Healing. This practice involves directing heartfelt intentions and energy towards someone in need. The remarkable aspect is that this simple act often yields positive outcomes.

Sending love energy doesn't necessitate expertise; rather, it's rooted in genuine care for another human being. Observing distressing news, such as a tragic loss, prompts heartfelt expressions like "I hope they will be okay," inadvertently channeling positive energy to those affected. The potency lies in the authenticity of the sentiment. The recipient, in ways inexplicable, receives this outpouring of love energy.

Consider encounters with individuals seeking assistance on the roadside. Instead of judgment, offering goodwill, even energetically, can make a difference. As a Reiki Master, incorporating sacred symbols like "Dai-Ke-Myo" and "Cho-Ku-Rei" intensifies the healing intention. While these symbols traditionally hold broader meanings, infusing them with intent empowers you as the creator of love and energy.

In the realm of long-distance healing, the use of Reiki symbols is prominent. Commencing with the "Hon-Sha-Ze-Sho-Nen" symbol, symbolizing long-distance healing, envisioning the symbols in your hand and projecting them towards the recipient enhances the process. Coupling this with the "Cho-Ku-Rei" symbol activates the transmission of love and energy.

Personal experiences affirm the effectiveness of sending Reiki symbols. Reports of heightened energy levels and even disturbances in sleep patterns indicate the impact. While Reiki symbols contribute significantly (providing 85% more energy), the fundamental essence is love and positive intent.

Practicing distant healing with others, mutually acknowledging the exchange of love, strengthens the process. Recipients often sense tingling sensations or chills, especially around the head or arms. This interactive approach, even without Reiki symbols, is both engaging and effective.

Engaging in joint practices with a partner can yield powerful results. Even in moments of distraction, the transmission of energy can be palpable. This emphasizes the principle that, while Reiki symbols enhance the process, the core requirement is an abundance of sincere and loving energy.

9 SPIRITUAL POWER

Isn't this interesting? I have believed in my guides because of my mother who believed that we have guides; some special beings who are celestial are invisible to the individuals' eyes, or some of us can hear them, feel them, or see them in our mind's eye. Please have an open mind.

How to Experience Your Loving Guides

Spirit guides are very positive beings.

if any entity, tells you or directs you to do something against your will or says anything negative or hurtful to you. They are not you're not Spirit guides.

For example, I was babysitting my grandson, whom I love with all my life, I was cutting some vegetables to cook for him. When all of a sudden, I heard a voice say inside my head, "stab him, just to know how it feels" it is not your spirit guide.

I said a prayer and told my guides to get rid of it.

Their common goal is to guide you back to alignment with your source (God), your higher self.

Or love for the universe or aiding in your life's work purpose.

Spirit guides or your angels will not tell you "that was a stupid thing you did" that is you or a mean spirit or other.

We are not alone, ever

To connect with your spirit guides. You must meditate or pray for them to appear to you in your dreams. Sometimes after meditation, you close your eyes, you will see sparkles of light or just bright lights like looking up at the stars on a bright night. These are how many guides, angels you may have at this time.

Some guides have helpers. But you have one main guide, the others are there to protect you depending on what your purpose is, military, warrior, police officer. It depends on your work purpose. Once you can get over the fear. They will come to you.

I saw my guides after two weeks of mediation because I was scared to meet them. But once I understood they love me and they were here for me. I saw one of them and he was the one that tried to make me laugh. He was very handsome. I also saw my other guide, she was a beautiful native girl, I got her name as well. That was like two weeks later. They will come, it depends on you. They don't want to scare you.

We the people, every one of us has our own spirit guides and angels. We are not meant to come by ourselves to this earth. Each of us has a series of guides and angels to help us with our purpose and assignments on this earthly journey. Our spirit guides do not violate free will or make choices for you or intervene in life's lessons.

When you want assistance from your guide, just ask, do have an open mind. You will sometimes hear the answer, receive it somehow and you will know, feel it, or hear it or receive a vision in your mind's eye. For example, I was wearing a jacket on a cool spring morning, I hung up my jacket. The next morning, I could not find the keys to my car.

I looked where I normally hang them and they were not there. I was very upset and yelled out to them. "Where are my car keys, you guys (guides) were with me! Tell me where they could be! In my mind's eye, I saw my jacket, I ran to the closet where I had all my winter jackets. There were my car keys.

I unconsciously placed them in my jacket in which I had put away in my winter closet. Which meant, I would not find them until the fall when I would use that certain jacket again. I was so grateful to them and I did let them know. I told them "I love them" and I felt a nice warmth come over me. To me it meant, they loved me too.

You don't have to wait to communicate with your guides only when you have problems or need them. You can converse with them. "Say thank you for leading you in the right direction. "Feel how their energy feels, how it feels to have them around you.

They have been around you since you were born, so the energy you may be feeling is so familiar, that you can't feel a difference, that is very true, but sometimes, I can feel a different or maybe warmer feeling for no reason at all.

Raising Your Vibration

Again, with the vibration, this is confusing to me, but maybe I am not the only one, Abraham Hicks quotes through Ester Hicks; "Love and appreciation are the identical vibrations. Appreciation is the vibration of alignment with who you are. Appreciation is the absence of everything that feels bad and the presence of everything that feels good."

"When you focus upon what you want and when you tell the story of how you want your life to be, you will come closer and closer to the vicinity of appreciation and when you reach it, it will pull you toward all these things that you consider to be good in a very powerful way."

Thank you, Abraham and Ester Hicks, I could listen to this lady forever, she is a very inspiring speaker. We need to hear her and others, like Tony Robinsons to only name a few.

Can this be much clearer? So, keeping yourself in the balance of being happy, feeling joy in your life. Letting go of unnecessary worrying, we worry about everything, Things that do not pertain to us. In another chapter, I wrote about keeping ourselves happy and joyful is a 24/7 job.

Saying a sweet prayer to our angels or spirit guides who are with you day and night, every second of every minute of every day of every week of every year, and so on. Just be grateful for having enough money to pay our rent to keep a roof over our heads, food on your table, paying our other bills. Wake up every day just to effect and give others a smile of a happy face.

Using our love vibration, some will give us a smile back. Sometimes, we make a remark to a person about how nice they look in that blouse they chose to wear. This makes the other person feel good about themselves as well. Been positive about what kind of day you want to have. Putting on an outfit that makes you feel confident. Doing what it takes to feel good about yourself. Share the smile.

We really have many things t be grateful for. Sometimes there are lessons we have to learn in this life. Pray that you "get " the lesson fast enough not to suffer too long.

Now that we know what our vibration is, keeping ourselves "upbeat" things will be more positive for us and your wish to come true is the universe and the universe is your genie. Be careful what you wish for, and be very specific. My mom would tell me a story about a person with a crippled hand who prayed to have his hand be just like the other one and one day he woke up with his other hand just like the other one, crippled as well. Be specific.

So, when asking for something you want, be very specific about what you want. Say "I ask for these things or equivalents, according to free will harming no one and for the good of all." I know you will be pleasantly surprised by what comes.

Wishing and Manifesting

We are always saying "I wish this I wish that" and when you get it, you were not specific enough. "Let's say you want a fluffy "dog to play with for your birthday, to have as a companion and someone says" I got you a puppy". But it turns out it is a stuffed little puppy; that barks and walks with you, a toy. You were not clear and specific enough that you wanted a real "live" puppy.

Maybe, this is a wrong example, but when you wish for something, the universe will get you what you asked for. But you have to be specific enough to get what you wish for. Another way of manifesting is to visualize yourself in a joyful, fulfilling lets' say relationship.

Make a list of what you want your partner to be and what character, mannerisms, and what it is you would like him to have as in humor, personality, and so on. Hold the list between your hands and pray into the list.

If you know Reiki, place the symbols into the list using the Sei-He-Ki and the Cho-Ku-Rei. Do your meditation and place the list under your lighted candle. Do this from a full moon to a new moon. This will add to the energy of what you are wishing for. Remember to be careful of what you wish for.

Do the same with a wish list of any kind. A new car, a new house. Do not limit yourself. Thinking this is all I can afford is limiting yourself, go all out.

See yourself in a new home with the keys in your hand. Hold the list between your hands and meditate.

If you know the Reiki symbols, use the Cho-Ku-Rei and double it using your image from your third eye to manifest it. Using affirmations can be more powerful. Phrase it by using the following affirmation:

"I ask for these things, or their equivalents or better, according to free will, harming none, and for the good of all." Using this affirmation can be revised to fit almost any situation. Using this gives your wish list and manifesting more positive intent and positive energy. This also corrects any ethical mistakes.

I used this confirmation from the Diane stein workbook. Lots of wonderful tools in that book.

If you are wishing or manifesting for someone who is in a relationship, or in such a way that deprives someone, it is unethical. It will not work. If you will hurt some else who is involved with another person. This could be that they are together because it is in their cards, destiny.

In asking for a job, for example, it is wrong to ask for someone else's job. Ask instead for the best-paying and pleasing job for you. Another way is to remember there are other ways to manifest things. By using your angels and spiritual beings that are available to you. Pray and petition to our Mother Goddess Azna, you don't necessarily have to believe in her. Just be willing to try her out. You'll see.

Do You Believe in Saints?

In my upbringing my parents prayed to saints, the Virgin of Santa Juanita, she was prayed to protect our newly born children and protect the pregnant moms or babies in the wound. The virgin Mary, the Virgin de Guadalupe. Mexican saint of all Mexico. Saint Teresa of Avila, there are just too many to mention. Do you believe in Saints? Maybe some don't know what they are.

Saints are often shown or painted with halos as symbols of holiness. Do you favor one? Some religions believe all those who have died, are saints. We were taught to pray to the saints we believed in.

If we don't believe in praying to them why the prayer to Mary, earthly mother of Jesus, of course, the Catholic church tells us to pray the" Hail Mary prayer". Some of the other religions and some churches still believe in Saints, I do not hear very much about saints anymore.

As I understand this "the Hail Mary" prayer is not a prayer of worship but a prayer of making a request. This justification for asking Mary in prayer is once again found in the Bible. Revelation 5:8 "The prayer of saints "being placed before the altar of God in heaven".

We, mainly my mom, who was a devoted Catholic member. Had us pray all the time. Pray to the saints, she had them everywhere around the house. Sometimes, I preferred to go to church, it was less time of kneeling at church. But if working took our time from going to church, mom would have us pray to all the saints.

That tradition of using saints and prayer to them is now gone with the grandparents who are now dead. I did not teach my kids to pray to the saints. We belonged to a church that did not believe in worshiping idols. So, can you see my conflictions here.?.

What does all this have to do with Curandera's magical stuff? Well, some of these saints are used to put a hack on someone like a curse. Or have someone placed in apposition where they won't be able to have sex with another person other than the wife or the husband.

Saints can help in doing good things, just like praying to God Jehovah or Mother Azna, who is unknown to many people. I understand she was removed from the bible because she was a woman. The translators of the bible and the inspired by godly men did not feel women could be prophets or placed in other holy powerful positions probably due to the fact of their monthly bleeding.

Now you know just how long all this oppression has been and continues in some countries up to this date, who can we blame? Things have not changed too much has it? Women of high positions may be able to change things, but change has to start with us. Right?

"A strong woman feels deeply and loves fiercely. Her tears flow as abundantly as her laughter. A strong woman is both soft and powerful, she is both practical and spiritual. A strong woman in her essence is a gift to the world." This is an unknown quote, but very powerful.

Saints are what we are taught for them to be. You don't hear very much of them anymore, so does that mean they don't exist? I will leave this up to your discretion.

How to Hear Your Angels

I just cannot say enough about our angels. They speak to us all the time and show us stuff we might be thinking of. It just so happens someone talks about what you have been thinking of or wondering. You may be seeing it in something you are reading. There are just too many coincidences. Have you thought it may be your angels trying to relay you a message? Are you hearing your angels and dismissing them?

I talked earlier about hearing some whispering or talking when no one is around and it might be a mental condition? Yet, when we listen to the voice of an angel or the voice of God, It's the sanest sound we will ever hear.

Chances are that you have heard your angels or other spiritual begins speak to you throughout your life. You could have a special gift or not. You don't need a special gift to hear your angels, guides, or other special beings.

Here are some special happenings that could have happened to you, and you did not even realize it.

You hear someone say something you needed to hear to solve an issue or a challenge. You don't even think about who said it, all you cared about was you resolved the problem from hearing that statement or listening in on a conversation. You hear a song or hear it repeatedly in your head.

There are many other examples that I am sure you have experienced and placed aside. Not that we really don't believe this could happen to us, but maybe you feel unworthy talking to your angels or why they would even bother talking to you in the first place if you don't even go to church?

Sometimes there is a RINGING in one ear. Sometimes the ringing is accompanied by a pulling of the ear lope or pinching, if this happens, they really want your attention.

If this happens tell them to please speak clearly. I have gotten this from my clients. I have to explain that you automatically have angels and guides. They came along with you when and since you were born.

You were aware of them back then, but they disappeared later in your life. They were and will always be there for you. Many people don't realize that and they could help you if you just ask. I got myself into some trouble at my job that could have gotten me fired. I didn't realized the extreme of it until it was brought to my attention by my supervisor.

I got down on my knees and prayed to God, my guides and my angels. The next day, my supervisor's, supervisor said, "No I understand where she was coming from and her way of processing her steps." I was spared. Thanks to my heavenly intervention. Plus, I loved my job and I was one of the top rankings of the state.

Too many times I had been short of money to pay my bills and out of the blue, after prayer to my guides and angels, I had just enough to pay my bills. I was always "grateful" for my blessings.

You'll be surprised where answers come from and when the results will just fall in your lap. It is a blessing from the guides and your angels to be served by them. They are waiting for you to acknowledge them. They are at your service.

Have you heard of Mother Goddess Azna? I had not heard of her until I read a book that Sylvia Brown wrote on her. Apparently, she is known by other names. Mother God has been trying to get our attention by coming to earth in other female forms.

More Things Angels Can Do

There are more things your angels can do. I have sent my angels to my relatives to heal them. I just ask them "to assist their guides/angels to speed their recovery. My daughter had gotten serious aches and pains, fever, and was having a hard time breathing, she stated it felt like someone was sitting on her chest. I send my guides and Reiki guides to assist in her healing.

We/I thought it could have been a virus that had spread throughout the whole world. My Daughter went to her doctor. He told her to come in quickly. Took a test to check for the popular virus. It turned out negative for the popular virus. I give credit to my Reiki angels and my guides. I have used my angels in that way ever since I received them from my Reiki attunements.

I was given more guides to work with. I use them to send healing to everyone who needs them. Family, friends, to people all over the world. We can send our angels everywhere. To take care of those who are in our prayers.

I trust my angels and guides; they also assist me with my intuition. If you need to help someone who does really understand what they are going through, ask your Reiki guides, the angels, your personal guides, "Ascending Masters", for help and listen, feel, or see the answer in a vision. always say thank you after a session.

I also use them in my Curandera sessions. I have them connect to my client's guides for guidance, and have their guides connect to my guides, and angels to receive help in healing them. This always works, I do this often enough that I forget to ask, just tell them my intentions.

Telling your guides or angels thank you is very important. I also use my guides, to help my clients after they leave and go home. I connect to their guide/s or angels to check on them. Sometimes, I get confirmations, which, I gratefully appreciate. We all need that validation. I know I do. My Angels always come through for me. I love that.

It helps me to know that they are real. Another thing is "you're never alone" You can talk to them 24/7 they do not sleep. You may need sleep, but they don't. What does this mean? Send them to work on someone.

Let's say you are having trouble with someone at work that is giving you a bad time. Send them Reiki with love to their guides, they will give that person love from you. If you are sincere, you will see the difference in them the next day at work. That will just as well, leave you alone, no comment, Maybe, a "hello" and will probably make themselves feel like the "big person" and let things be.

The symbols are the essence and formula of Rciki. They are the keys to using and passing on this healing system. Reiki is an extremely simple method of healing. Once you learn the symbols and healing methods, you can make them and use them positively in any type of healing.

Remember, what is send out returns to you, good or ill. The intent to harm anyone returns to you. The intent to harm someone with this system designed for healing whether it succeeds or not, becomes part of the karma of the sender. By the intention to do good overrides any loss of information. By doing your best with positive intentions, your Reiki methods. You can make them and use them positively in any type of healing.

Mother Goddess Azna

Like many famous females like the Blessed Mother Lourdes and La Virgin de Guadalupe, or known as the lady of Guadalupe, the Mexican Lady of protection. Mother Azna has been trying to get our attention for centenaries. Mother Azna is an emotional and sensing Goddess.

Mother Azna works out of the heart; she listens to our prayer and gives you a quicker response than Father God. Because Father God has the intellect and not the emotional being.

Sylvia takes us into a journey where she discusses the supersession of Mother Goddess by the male-dominated politics of modern-day religious dogma. The bible was written by those men. They could not believe a female could have that much power. So, they left her out and kept us in the dark about her.

In the bible, it does say "let's make them in our image, male and female. I have talked to priests and some ministers about her they know nothing of such thing. Some did not believe that she even existed, When Father God was talking about "we" as in" we will make them in our image", in the bible he was talking to Christ, not Mother Goddess.

I first learned of her through Sylvia's books, the book is dedicated just to Mother God. In her book, Sylvia shows to petition her in prayer.

Here is the following prayer.

AZNA'S PRAYER

"We give homage to You, Blessed Mother Azna, because of our love for you and because of your love for us. Thank you for the grace and protection You have given us, Beloved Mother. We know You have ultimate power, glory, and righteousness. No matter what comes our way, we know You are there for us with Your sword in hand to protect us from the darkness.

You, Mother Azna, have the loving emotional power to intercept and create miracles. Your understanding and love are boundless, and with You, anything is possible. I ask You, Beloved Mother, to grant my petition today…..(state petition)….. We know You will not forget us or leave us. We feel Your glorious presence, knowing You are with us today, tomorrow, and always, ever grateful for your constant, eternal love. I ask this in the Name of God the Mother, the Father, and the Holy Child, Amen."

When the world was created Mother Azna was there. Mother Anza was the creator of mostly all of it. Mother Azna, is that why the world is so colorful? It's beautifully covered in love and color. Upon the earth and especially under the sea.

I truly believe that Mother Azna exits. I use her in my Curandera healings as well. I used a petition for her blessings in this way. I wrote what I wanted on a piece of paper, placed it in a little metal cup read it to her, and burned it. I had forgotten I had done that and my petition was answered. You try a petition and see for yourself. I recommend you keep a copy of the petition. I had forgotten of other things I had petitioned to her and received that too. But had forgotten I had petitioned it from Mother Azna. The choice is yours.

10 CURANDERO THERAPY PRACTICE

I used to work with the Behavioral Mental Health agency and Being Latina, I wanted to mention to everyone that, If I would get the opportunity to work with mental health, and would have liked to integrate the psychotherapy and curanderismo into our mental health services to better serve the Latino community.

Psychotherapy and Curanderismo

As you read the Curandero book, you will find that the Latino people believe in many magical and spiritual beliefs that they apply to everyday life. Those Latinos raised with Mexican grandparents and al Estilo Mexicano, come with many beliefs. "Curando con un huevo" for example, pretty much takes care of many illnesses.

While I worked at mental health, I had some Latinos clients who would complain about not having a person who understood the Latino culture. "They find things to diagnosis me as something when I would tell them "I felt I have been cursed, or that I felt that I had an attachment. "Like an evil spirit."

Psychiatrists, are mainly Caucasian or of another ethnicity. There is Latino therapist, but I have found that they will comply with the western methods of counseling. I mentioned this complaint to the therapist and psychiatrist, psychologist, and those in charge of the mental health like the commissioners.

They agreed with me, but they stated they had trouble finding people who had qualifications. They would find those who spoke Spanish or some form of the Spanish language, but in my experience, they did not understand the Curandero aspect part of the Latinos. Hispanics seek help on how to face life's challenges.

I would recommend my clients to the Spanish-speaking professionals but were not satisfied with the comprehension of the culture. The service providers in the traditional system of mental health do not thoroughly understand the cultural needs of the Hispanic psychological disorders

One Psychiatrist even got upset with me. I was trying to explain the differences in our beliefs and how some of the tactics which they use, for example, "what does the following mean to you?" "If you live in a glass house you shouldn't throw rocks." Who understands this?

One of my clients I worked with had no choice but to stay with a psychologist even though the Psychologist spoke Spanish, but who would get upset at my client and give him a higher dose of medication.

My client would tell me he did not take the high doses. My client understood he needed to stay on his medication, but would not take the higher doses. He was trying to hold on to a job, but the higher doses would interfere with his functioning.

I have read and heard that other Latinos have had the same complaints. But in California, I read that many professionals are having more of an understanding of the need of combining both curanderismo and psychotherapy, they are about the same in using talk therapy and advice seeking.

My desire is that someday the alternative healing rituals and therapeutic techniques of the Latino culture-based system of care can be integrated into the western therapeutic practice to elicit more successful mental health integration for a better outcome for the Latino patients with mental health issues.

Using Hypnotherapy

Curandero therapy is something I enjoy working with because of the interesting and exciting things my clients appear to learn about themselves. Why? Because there is more freedom in using hypnotherapy, to me, it is like a magical method. I used hypnosis with a client that feared losing her husband.

She sincerely felt that every time he would step out that door, he would never come back. This lady would break down in tears just worrying about him. She felt that was not right. Her family would tease her for feeling this way about a man, having had so many boyfriends before settling for this one in particular.

I thought maybe she was just co-dependent on her husband for her happiness. This client I thought at first that she had bad relationships and experiences with men she had encounters, Ok I thought let's start there. After asking some questions that I felt she could tell me more, I was not getting anywhere. no? OK.

Sometimes, when you're trying to help people, asking questions and the right questions really helps. But when people have no clue as to why they are having such problems. I go to hypnotherapy. Some people are afraid of it because they have heard negative stories about being under hypnosis, she expressed to me that she had heard that a spirit could take over their subconscious or an earthbound.

Negative stories that are not always true. It happens that when a therapist using hypnosis could change your life, good for the person, but maybe bad for the family or significant other. I had a client that changed, he was more aware of things happening around him. He later found out his wife was using black magic on him. Anyway, that's another story.

I explained, that because we could not find a cause for that, it could be a past life that was causing this unknown reason. We decided to give it a try, Using some practice we started the process. Using motel room doors to check in to one of the rooms her angels and guides would guide her to choose a door. I explained the protection she had.

Told her we could use her belief in Christ for protection. It made her more comfortable for me to use Christ for her protection, (just in case) she felt much better. This is one of the processes I use is to make the client more comfortable and by using their beliefs. I used the process of choosing doors like at a hotel.

What color was the door? Place hand on the doorknob, how does the doorknob feel like? What is its shape, round, or handle? Open the door, and take a step in, knowing you are being protected by Christ, Go back as far as it takes?

What do you see, is it day or night? "Day time" What is happening, "I see children and I am their father," How do you know this? Because they are saying "goodbye daddy" "my wife is making me promise I will come back. We both are crying and I promised. I must be male," Look at your shoes, what do they look like? "Boots" I am wearing a uniform, I must be going to war" I am holding a rifle."

Ok, let go forward in time. At the count of 3 Let's go to another Signiant point in that life. 1 -2-3 your further in This life, what is happening? I'm in pain, I have been shot, and the light is fading, I believe I am dying." Let's take you out of this pain, at my count of 3. 1-2-3-! Do you see a white light? "Yes, But it is above me. Now, I am in a room, and there is a lot of light around me.

I continue to be in pain, only I recognize this pain, I am giving birth, I believe I am having a baby," My husband is crying and saying to me. " Honey, you are losing a lot of blood. Please don't leave me alone." I hear a baby crying and now I cannot hear the baby, I am scared," It's dark" and Client is crying intensely, so I bring her out, using Christ as her protector. Brought her back to the room, to her lying down in my office. Calmed her and asked what she remembered.

The client describes saying "goodbye" and the pain and fears it caused her to feel like the one leaving for war. The last thing she remembers is seeing his wife in his mind, Crying. But when I was giving birth, I remember seeing the face of a person crying again for me and I think I died again. But it felt like the same kind of deep love".

Does this feel familiar to you in this life? "Does this mean I am going to die, or am I going to lose my husband?" This could mean that now that you know why you feel this way, it will stop. You will no longer feel like you will lose him because that person was you. When we learn our lessons or reasons why. What did each person in those lives ask you? One made you promise what?

"To promise her that I would be back, the other, well, he did not want me to leave him alone…" in your heart you did not want to do this, but you had no control. Only Christ was there for you so that you could understand, it's OK. How do you feel about this?

"I was afraid at first, but now, I feel it is all in Christ's hands, and I should just leave it in his hands." Curandera: " And now that, you know that it was you who was always leaving, how do you feel about that?" Client: " Am I the one who is going to die?" Curandera: " No one makes it out alive while living on earth, we all die, some time or another, even of old age."

It took a couple more sessions, but she does not fear, in the same way, knowing her husband is fine. She invited her husband to come into a session with us. Her husband teased this lady by saying she is crazy or she really loves me. My client no longer feels this fear, she feels it's other things now. Wants to learn why by using hypnotherapy? I created a person who feels Hypnosis is the only way to go.

Sleep/Relaxation Induction

Sleeping is a very important habit to get into. Sleep is a very important life necessity. I do not have to remind you of all kinds of things that could go wrong, especially if you're a surgeon, a transportation driver, airline operator. Lack of sleep affects our lives in every way.

Here are some tips that could help:

- Do not drink caffeine or alcohol before bedtime.
- Some claim that alcohol helps you fall asleep, but it affects the REM (rapid eye movement) deep sleep symptoms.
- Open your mouth slightly, when trying to sleep.
- Create an environment for sleeping in your sleeping area. No bright lights, no lights if that makes a difference to you. Keep it dark.
- I have even found that changing old pillows, for new ones, help.
- Aromatherapy like lavender, sage, Indian Shrinivas burning scents light scents,, some have a very positive light sense. Promotes relaxation.
- Create a non-stimulant atmosphere or what you would consider an ideal environment in your bedroom for sleeping.
- Listen to relaxing music.
- If you still can't sleep, get up and read
- Do not stay in bed if you are still can't sleep.
- Hide the clock or cover it with something that helps hide it or dim its light.

Sleep induction script

Let's start by tightening your eyebrow muscles by raising your eyebrows, now count to 6

in your mind and say to yourself "relax and sleep".

Squint your eye tightly shut, count to 6 in your mind, and say to yourself, "relax and sleep".

Tighten your jaw, by biting down on your teeth, count to 6 in your mind and say to yourself," relax and sleep".

Lift your shoulders muscles, hold for the count of 6 in your mind. Say to yourself, relax and sleep".

Tilt your neck, again count to 6 in your mind let your neck fall on your pillow and relax the muscles in your neck and say "relax and sleep. Now, give yourself permission to fall asleep. If not, go on with the rest of your body. arche your back again hold to the count of 6 in your mind, and say" relax and sleep." Lift your arms and hold them to the count of 6 in your mind, now lay them by your side and say "relax and sleep".

Continue with clenching your hands into a fist, as tight as your can, count to 6 in your mind and let go moving and relaxing your fingers, and say repeating to yourself "relax and sleep". "Relax and sleep". If you sleep on your side, turn yourself to your sleeping position. And sleep. Sleep….sleep…

Still not sleepy, continue with your anus, tighten it, to the count of 6 in your mind and say. "Relax and sleep." Next, tighten your legs as if stretching them hold to the count of 6 in your mind. Say to yourself. "Relax and sleep". Do the same with your toes, curl your toes intensively, count to 6 in your mind. Say to yourself. Relax and sleep. Still not sleepy, make yourself yawn. Yawn again take, a total of 3 yawns. Turn to your sleeping position and relax deeply and sleep.

Repeat this process as needed. You can also record this process on your phone or other device and as you fall asleep, the recording will turn itself off. You could add relaxing music to the recording, as well.

SWEET DREAMS!

ABOUT THE AUTHOR

Rosa M Luna is a highly esteemed retired mental health professional and a licensed clinical hypnotherapist in the State of Oregon, bringing a wealth of experience and compassion to her holistic healing practices. Her academic journey has been marked by studies at Treasure Valley Community College, complimented by a diverse range of educational experiences that have enriched her understanding of the intricate nuances of mental health and well-being.

As a committed advocate for holistic healing, Rosa is a practicing Reiki Master, harnessing the transformative power of energy healing. She is also a founding member of the prestigious Luna Institute of Curanderos, a testament to her dedication to curandero therapy and its profound impact on mental and emotional wellness.

Beyond her extensive clinical background, Rosa plays a pivotal role as an Olympian Life Coach and instructor at St. Paul's Free University, where she imparts her vast knowledge and experience to the next generation of professionals. Her commitment to education and mentorship underscores her belief in the importance of sharing wisdom to foster growth and understanding in the field.

An accomplished author and speaker, Rosa M Luna has devoted her career to facilitating mental and emotional well-being. Her multifaceted contributions have made a lasting impact on the field of mental health and holistic healing, leaving an indelible mark on the lives she has touched. Through her innovated approaches and unwavering commitment to the holistic healing journey, Rosa continues to inspire and empower individuals toward a path of greater mental and emotional wellness.

For more information, visit: www.rosamluna.com

www.ingramcontent.com/pod-product-compliance
Lightning Source LLC
Chambersburg PA
CBHW070812280726
48660CB00015B/412